Countermemory

COUNTERMEMORY

A Rhetoric of Resistance

April L. O'Brien
and James Chase Sanchez

The University of Alabama Press
Tuscaloosa

The University of Alabama Press
Tuscaloosa, Alabama 35487-0380
uapress.ua.edu

Typeface: Adobe Caslon Pro

Cover image: Vdant85/stock.adobe.com

Cover design: Sandy Turner Jr.

Cataloging-in-Publication data is available from the Library of Congress.
ISBN: 978-0-8173-2225-0 (cloth)
ISBN: 978-0-8173-6188-4 (paper)
E-ISBN: 978-0-8173-9547-6

To the people who inspire me most: Mike, Emma, and Noah. I love you all to the moon and back.

—April

To Katie: Thanks for always inspiring me to do my best work.

—James

Contents

Figures

Preface

An Education

April

I encountered the faintest notion of countermemory over a decade ago. Before I tell that story, though, it is important to communicate how deeply I was entrenched in dominant cultural narratives for many years. I want to relay this information for two reasons: First, I identify as a white settler who writes, researches, and teaches about issues of racism, countermemory, and social justice. There is an obvious dissonance between my identity and the focus of my scholarship, and in the spirit of transparency, I need to address this gap and to acknowledge the labor of the many Black, Latinx, Indigenous, and other marginalized scholars whom I cite in this book. Truly, these individuals have risked much and given much. As someone who does not "live at the intersection of oppression," it is my goal "to approach change-making with humility" (Walton, Moore, and Jones 2019, 134). Second, I think about the readers of this book, many of whom might share a similar identity and background. It is my hope that some of those readers will recognize themselves in this story and will consider the value in what James and I argue.

As I mentioned, this concept—countermemory—originated many years ago. It started when I discovered that most everything I had ever been taught about race, racism, American history, and whiteness was false. After finishing my BA, I took several years off and then returned to higher education to pursue a certification in secondary education. Since I already had a degree in English, I just needed to take a handful of undergraduate and graduate courses in education for this postbaccalaureate degree. One course, Historical and Philosophical Forces Influencing Secondary Education, is responsible for the shift in my entire perspective. I sat in the basement classroom of Ketchum Hall at Buffalo State College day after day and learned about systemic racism as it impacted residential segregation, the construct of race, the privileges associated with whiteness, Native American "boarding schools" just miles away from campus, inequities in education, cultural capital, and many other concepts. While I did not learn specifically about countermemory, I did become aware of whiteness as a system that informed the way history is communicated. I became aware of the lies that I had been taught about the United States, both in the classroom and in the public sphere. I realized for the first time how these dominant cultural narratives seek to erase any information that does not align with their established goal: to maintain white supremacy at all costs. For example, when I was educated about Native American tribes in New York State in elementary and middle/high school, the subject was always approached from the perspective of white colonizers. There was little, if any, discussion about the immorality of colonization, much less the slaughter of millions of Indigenous people so white men could establish their own homes. And there was certainly no information provided about Native "boarding schools," many of which existed just a few miles from my home outside of Buffalo, New York. Through the system of these schools, young Indigenous people were forced to leave their homes, abandon their languages and cultures, be separated from their parents and siblings, all so white men could teach them how to be "civilized" (Douglas 2013).

In the same class, when we watched the docuseries *Race: The Power of an Illusion* during class time, I was introduced to the ways in which American culture normalized categorizing people according to skin color and how nineteenth-century science legitimized these beliefs. From the final episode of the docuseries, "The House We Live In," I learned about residential segregation, and the role the Federal Housing Administration played in preventing Black Americans from securing mortgages. Concepts like redlining and the racial wealth gap were unfamiliar prior to taking the course, and the more I researched about these examples of structural racism, the more I realized that this information had been purposely kept from me in all the education I had received previously. Since I attended a nearly all-white private school during my elementary and secondary education years and a nearly all-white private, liberal arts college for my undergrad, it is not surprising that I was never exposed to this information about racism in the United States. That semester, I had two choices. I could either withdraw from this new information and refuse to acknowledge my complicity in systemic racism, or I could address my privilege and work collectively with others to understand oppression and spur change. I chose the latter. This choice does not make me a superstar in any way; rather, as a white woman with considerable privilege and power, it is the very least I can do. More directly related to the topic of this current book, that semester, I learned that a dominant narrative existed and that more people needed to learn about its counternarrative, what I now call countermemory. While I did not return to this seedling of an idea until a few years later it was a concept that emerged as both a personal and scholarly endeavor.

When I left Western New York for rural South Carolina, I moved to a historic town called Pendleton. After living there for a few months, I discovered that the town held ghost tours, weddings, and other social engagements in the local plantation houses. In Pendleton, a historic town celebrating 225 years of existence (at the time of my residency), it became apparent that the Lost Cause ideology permeated all aspects of public memory and tourism. The town also overtly erased Black history from its public memory, both in terms of recounting the significant Black individuals and organizations and in terms of any truth-telling efforts about the role that slavery, Reconstruction violence, and Jim Crow has played in the town's identity and development. I realized again that a dominant narrative existed and that people (me included) needed to be educated about countermemories of Pendleton. Thanks to the kindness of a few Black Pendletonians, I was able to collect oral histories and explore the town's Black history archives. This project was the birth of my scholarship on countermemory. I initiated an introductory engagement with countermemory in "Composing Counter-Memories: Using Memorial and Community Engagement to Disrupt Dominant Narratives," and touched on the concept with other articles. Yet, it was not until James and I discovered our overlapping research interests and became friends that countermemory truly emerged as a rhetorical construct in our article, "Racial Countermemory." Between my experiences in Buffalo and Pendleton, and James's perspective as a person of color who grew up in a small Texas town, the concept of countermemory became something more than just an academic pursuit.

James

My introduction to countermemory stems from a similar situation to April's but is a bit more complex. In my hometown of Grand Saline, Texas, the legacies of race and racism are enshrined in the community's very being. The townspeople tell stories about their unique history of racism, pride themselves on their bigoted histories, and still have no Black families within the city limits. In 2014, Charles Moore, an elderly man who was raised in Grand Saline during the 1940s and 1950s, drove to the town and self-immolated in the Dollar General parking lot. He left a note on his windshield calling for the town to repent of their white supremacist histories and present and to try and be more inclusive. I have written about Charles Moore and Grand Saline extensively in my monograph, *Salt of the Earth: Rhetoric, Preservation, and White Supremacy* (2021), and illustrated the pathologies racist discourse in my documentary, *Man on Fire*. I will not rehash here what some readers may know. But even as I have adopted autoethnographic methodologies and employed the critical race theory lens and racial rhetorics to better understand these events, I keep being drawn back to what invited me into this scholarship when Moore died: racialized public memory.

The memories Charles Moore expressed in his letter to the town—naming the KKK meetings and a lynching that occurred in the outskirts of the community—happened thirty or forty years before I was born and forty or fifty years before

I moved to Grand Saline. However, I could not escape the fact that the stories he described, the stories he died for, paralleled my own memories of the town in the early- to mid-2000s. I heard about lynchings of yesteryear (or, on some occasions, myths of more contemporary lynchings). I was told the KKK still met on the outskirts of town. I knew the exact stories that Moore had died for. Our memories were the same.

Most residents of Grand Saline publicly disagree with Moore's memories and my own. Soon after his death, numerous townspeople wrote a letter to the *Grand Saline Sun* newspaper editor, claiming that Moore had been away from town for a long time and did not have the facts right (they also disposed of the editor after she agreed with Moore's perception of the town). On social media, former friends and family of friends called me a race-baiter, accusing me of lying and betraying the town, and labeled me as a "pseudo academic" for being public about Moore's death. Though I knew my memories were real, they were my own. While a few people messaged me privately to agree with me, there was not enough public momentum for a real conversation to take place about my hometown's history and perception of itself.

While doing research for my book, however, I came across a story that seemed to agree with me and Moore. In 1909, the editor of the *Grand Saline Sun* wrote an article claiming that in the post-Reconstruction era, a Black massacre had occurred in the town when Black people moved in to work during the salt mine's labor strike. He wrote that if you were to drain one of the ponds on the edge of town, the bones would cover the pond's entire floor. While that seems like an embellishment (has anyone ever looked?), the local county historian Elvis Allen flat out dismisses it as someone trying boost newspaper sales. Maybe Allen is right. Maybe not. Either way, the legacy of racism in Grand Saline has existed since at least 1909. Moore had memories of racism forty years later. Mine occurred more than a century after that first article was published.

This framework—why my and Moore's memories were so different from those of the rest of the town, or more so than they would acknowledge—fascinates me. It feels as if an entire community is gaslighting me. Had the ten years between moving away from Grand Saline to writing about my experiences there reshaped my memories? Was I just exaggerating my memories to make them more enthralling? Was I a liar? These questions contrasted with recollections of called "Wetback" and "Beaner" by high schoolers, learning about stories of Black people being decapitated, hearing the football chant "we're all right 'cuz we're all white," and other racist memories. These memories have lived within me for nearly twenty years now. I know they are true because of how many people acknowledge them in private.

Of course, the reason why the community vehemently disagrees with me publicly is not just because my memories could hurt their reputation, though that is part of the reason. They also do it because my memories counter their own. While they want to imagine themselves as a safe, nonracist, rural haven, my stories and Moore's confront their memory caverns. Our memories challenge how they fashion themselves. They indicate that something darker lurks beneath the surface of the community's old-fashioned, "y'all-are-welcome-here" veneer. Our memories thus become dangerous in that they have the capability of publicly cultivating a different side of the Grand Saline. As a rhetorician, I am fascinated by how the community has perceived and responded to these memories.

Countermemory, based on a theory-driven definition that will be discussed in the introduction, expresses narratives and histories that a specific community has either chosen not to remember or forgets (often willfully but not always). In the case of Grand Saline, the story of Charles Moore and the town's racism does not feel like something the town has simply forgotten over the years and decades. There is a deliberate desire to forget, to move past dark realities that would be hard to face. Grand Saline does not want to remember. Still, many of the acts that Moore and I carried out would be considered acts of countermemory (even though I am sure neither one of us would refer to them as such at the moment). Moore's letter and his self-immolation, for instance, would be acts attempting to get the town to remember and discuss their racist history. My book and documentary about Moore are also acts of countermemory, ones that indicate the town's consistent cover-up modus operandi needs to change. Therefore, the reason town members publicly chastise or discredit Moore and me is because they know we are agents of this countermemory. We represent something they want to ignore. We remind them of a past that exists even if they continue to deny it.

Acknowledgments

Writing this book has been a journey filled with challenges, triumphs, and invaluable support from many remarkable individuals. I extend my deepest gratitude to:

My friends and colleagues at Clemson University, Sam Houston State University, and elsewhere: I want to thank Victor Vitanza, Jan Holmevik, Cynthia Haynes, and Greg Ulmer. Without the creative space that you all created, I would have never been free enough to imagine a project like this. I'm thankful for my dearest colleagues at SHSU, including Xiaobo Belle Wang, Leslie Anglesey, Ada Hubrig, Shyam Pandey, Kristin Bennett, Brandon Strubberg, and Carroll Nardone. Thanks also to my department chair, Jacob Blevins, who has always supported my work in every way possible. I also want to thank the people who have become my dearest friends (even across the miles!) and who have inspired me as a scholar and teacher: Stephen Quigley, Mari Ramler, and Shauna Chung. I am changed for the better because of your presence in my life. I think of my extended academic family and thank Justin Hodgson, Jason Helms, and Laura Rosche for your kindness, support, and friendship.

In terms of institutional support that made this project possible, I am grateful to Sam Houston State University's new faculty grant, which provided funding for travel and technology to take photos, gather data, and repeatedly experience the sites that are central to this book. I also appreciate the departmental support for travel grants that allowed me to present research at various conferences throughout the writing of this book.

Thank you to our editor, Kristen Hop, for being so enthusiastic and supportive throughout this process. I always felt capable and supported, and I'm grateful for Kristen's role in my experience as a first-time book author.

I am forever grateful to my coauthor, James Chase Sanchez, for first connecting with me via Twitter years ago. We've collaborated on a few projects now (this being the largest!) and working with James has been a delight in every way. I'm so thankful for his experience, presence, and support as we've written this book together.

Finally, my biggest thanks of all is to my family. During the writing of this book, so much transpired. My parents moved to Texas, and then they moved in with us. We've taken care of them these last three and a half years, and now they are moving back north to live with other family members. It's been a gift to share a life together here in Texas. My kids have grown up throughout the writing of this book. During the early days, we were all home during COVID, and we all worked on our various assignments together. (My noise-canceling headphones should definitely receive the MVP during those days!) Thank you to Mike, who always listens to my ideas and supports my research with his whole heart.

This book wouldn't have been possible without each and every one of you.

—April L. O'Brien

I first want to thank my wife, Katie Runde Sanchez, for her love and support during this project. None of this would be possible without being able to bounce ideas off her during early morning coffee time, post-dinner chats, and various writing sessions. You always help me see the bigger picture.

Special thanks to colleagues Joshua Daniel, Terry Peterman, Tyler Branson, Carrie Helms, Alex Slotkin, Brad Lucas, and Charlotte Hogg. Our conversations over the past few years were foundational in the framing of this book. This research has been important to my connection to place, space, and home and has shifted my relationships with friends, family, and the field of writing and composition. I appreciate everyone for listening and engaging.

Middlebury College and its Writing and Rhetoric Program have afforded me ample opportunities to pursue this research in various pathways, and I am grateful for the one-on-one feedback from colleagues and broader discussions about this work. I especially appreciate the decision to delay my term as chair of the program until I was done with this work.

Lastly, thanks to my coauthor extraordinaire, April L. O'Brien, for this collaboration. We first had an in-person conversation about our interest in countermemory at the Conference on College Composition and Communication in 2019, and I will be forever appreciative of your expertise, tenacity, and thoroughness. You are the backbone of this book, and I am lucky to cowrite with such a caring person.

—James Chase Sanchez

Countermemory

Introduction

A Lion's History, or A New History of the Hunt

Until the lions have their own historians, the history of the hunt will always glorify the hunter.

—Chinua Achebe

The 1872 painting *American Progress*, by John Gast, visually represents Manifest Destiny, a dominant narrative about our nation's history that portrays white men as brave explorers and Native Americans as obstacles to westward expansion (fig. 1). Centered in the middle of the painting is a woman named "Progress" dressed in Grecian robes and leading the charge toward the West. The painting is split in thirds: two-thirds dominated by sunlight and the left one-third characterized by darkness and storm clouds. On the lighter side, Gast incorporates symbols of modernization, including telegraph poles, trains, stagecoaches, Conestoga wagons, bridges, and ships, along with images of farmers and miners moving toward the West. In fact, all movement is "Westward," or toward the left side of the painting. On the dark side, chaos looms, represented via sinister clouds, a mountain range, wild animals like buffalo and a growling bear, and a group of Native Americans fleeing toward the edge of the painting. The placement of the Native Americans near the snarling bear and running buffalo is intentional; these groups are viewed as threatening, wild, and barbaric—just like the animals. All are obstacles to American progress.

Gast's painting vividly demonstrates a dominant white narrative of "progress" in the United States, an ideology that countermemory, the subject of this book, seeks to dismantle. By identifying these dominant narratives, this book demonstrates how pervasive dominant white, hegemonic narratives have been—and continue to be—and the varied responses to these narratives in traditional public memory artifacts and sites, as well as within popular culture. In this book, we establish a rhetoric of liberatory countermemory, which we define as an organized movement to expose hegemonic, whitewashed historical accounts that have surged over the past ten to twenty years. Countermemory "critiques the silences" in public memory; it opposes, resists, and revises dominant public memory (Todd 2016, 17). More specifically, we interrogate what we term the "liberatory" side of countermemories, or countermemories that attempt to bolster histories of people of color and the oppressed in the United States.

Figure 1. John Gast's *American Progress*, 1872; Library of Congress Prints and Photographs Division, Washington, DC.

Gast's painting is not aberrant in its depiction of the history of the American West. Rather, this artifact represents an abiding narrative about the United States. In this narrative, white men are the victors (in fact, white men are the only "heroes" of the painting), and they are portrayed as driving the "darkness," including those with darker skin, off the page and out of history. People of color are communicated as dangerous, violent, and wild. In this dominant narrative, the history of the United States is one of progress, advancement, and improvement: "High school textbooks present a nation that has always been getting better, in everything from methods of transportation to race relations. We used to have slavery; now we do not. We used to have lynchings; now we do not. Baseball used to be all-white; now it is not. Step by step, race relations have somehow improved on their own, according to the textbooks' archetypal story line of constant progress, and the whole problem has now been fixed or is on the way to being fixed" (Loewen 2005, 24).

Tied to that narrative of progress is the notion that white men are responsible for all that is good and hopeful about the nation's history. As a counterpoint, white women and people of color are not a part of the dominant narrative. The experiences of Native Americans, Black Americans, Mexican American and Latinx people, Asian Americans, and all people of color are viewed as on the periphery of the "real" American story. In fact, in a recent interview, when questioned about the relevance of slavery to the country's historical identity, former speaker of the House Newt Gingrich responded in this manner: "I think certainly if you're an African American, slavery is at the center of what you see as the American experience, but for most Americans most of the time, there were a lot of other things going on" (Hains 2019). Gingrich's assessment of any narrative that counters the dominant one is commonplace. White Americans (who he just refers to as "Americans") prefer their version of history, and many have and will continue to directly oppose any formation of countermemory. Artifacts like *American Progress* are examples of public memory because "public memory is both attached to a past [. . .] and acts to ensure a future of further remembering of that same event" (Casey 2004, 17). While attached to the past, Gast's painting depicts sentiments of American identity that have circulated for the last 150 years.

However, Gingrich's statement makes certain knowledge claims about public memory in the United States. In his worldview, slavery is only relevant to Black Americans, and it is but a footnote in a history that centers the white experience for "everyone else." This is why, when questioned about whether Americans frame America as defined by racism, Gingrich called any movement to do so a lie (Hains 2019). This reaction is echoed around the nation by many white Americans when they are forced to confront public memory that exposes racism. In 2017, white supremacists marched through Charlottesville, Virginia, chanting "blood and soil!" (a callback to Nazi propaganda and nationalism) in response to the removal of Confederate monuments. When the National Memorial for Peace and Justice, commemorating those who were lynched in the United States, was built in Montgomery, Alabama, in 2018, many residents resented it, citing a fear that it would "dredge up the past and incite anger and backlash within black communities" (Levin 2019). One resident complained that it was "a waste of money, a waste of space [and was] bringing up bullshit" (qtd. in Levin 2019). The McLeod Plantation in Charleston, South Carolina, gallingly received negative feedback on Yelp and TripAdvisor because of what one visitor calls "a highly politicized" tour that focuses on "civil rights and slave suffrage" (@blorenzo 2019). Former Colorado congressional candidate Saira

Rao retweeted (and criticized) a two-star Google review of Whitney Plantation that said, in part, "My husband and I were extremely disappointed in this tour [. . .] We did not come to hear a lecture on how the white people treated slaves, we came to get this history of a southern plantation and get a tour of the house and grounds. The tour guide was so radical about slave treatment we felt we were being lectured and bashed about the slavery" (qtd. in Avery 2019). These examples demonstrate the extent to which many white people oppose countermemory in the heritage tourism industry, museums, and memorials.

Beside the examples already mentioned, a recent and more popular (digital) example of countermemory is the Pulitzer Prize–winning *1619 Project*, helmed by Nikole Hannah-Jones, which argues that the true birth of our nation is 1619, when a ship arrived at Point Comfort in the British colony of Virginia with a cargo of twenty to thirty enslaved Africans (Silverstein 2019). While 1776 has always been understood as the "birth" of our nation, *The 1619 Project* seeks to subvert that narrative with a new one—one that centers slavery as the foundation: "Out of slavery—and the anti-black racism it required—grew nearly everything that has truly made America exceptional: its economic might, its industrial power, its electoral system, its diet and popular music, the inequities of its public health and education, its astonishing penchant for violence, its income inequality, the example it sets for the world as a land of freedom and equality, its slang, its legal system and the endemic racial fears and hatreds that continue to plague it to this day. The seeds of all that were planted long before our official birth date, in 1776, when the men known as our founders formally declared independence from Britain" (Silverstein 2019). Establishing 1619 as the true beginning of the United States is an act of resistance. It rejects almost 250 years of a dominant history that commemorates generations of white men—a history that has been proclaimed by more white male historians—and creates a new timeline and a new center point. If 1619 is the new beginning for the United States, there are a host of implications that cannot be ignored or erased, such as the framing of slavery as more foundational to our country's beginning. Most importantly, *The 1619 Project* argues that slavery was not an unpleasant fluctuation in an otherwise noble, propitious, and heroic civilization. Rather, the tentacles of slavery reach deep within all aspects of American life, including the epidemic of mass incarceration, the persistence of residential and educational segregation, and the dramatic economic disparities that exist in our country. Slavery constitutes the United States.

Remembering various aspects of the United States' painful past is challenging because the act of remembrance collides with powerful narratives that are held by many Americans. While ideologies like the Lost Cause may be popular in some white circles in the US South, concepts like American exceptionalism are far more pervasive across the political spectrum and geographic regions.

American exceptionalism, while widely believed, is not a harmless belief. Rather, it shuts down the influence or circulation of liberatory countermemory because, at its core, American exceptionalism espouses a progressive idealization of the country. Put differently, because the United States is an "exceptional nation," blessed by God and different from all other countries in the world, it cannot also still contend with issues like systemic racism. Since the country continues to progress in its treatment of people of color, we must be careful to compartmentalize injustice and violence as something that occurred "back then" and to insist that racial issues have continued to improve over time. Thus, American exceptionalism prevents any forward progress even as it attempts to demonstrate the country's progress. There is no space for an honest accounting for countermemory because countermemory clashes with the belief that the country is special and always in a state of improvement toward greatness.

Thus, this book argues for a better understanding of a rhetoric of liberatory countermemory that rejects dominant cultural narratives and expands the stories and lived experiences of people of color in the United States. While we see countermemory as a theory and practice that extends to a variety of contexts, we focus primarily on countermemory in the American South, and by extension, countermemory that deals with Black, Latinx, and Indigenous individuals and histories. Within the context of this call for a rhetoric that acts, or what Natasha Jones and Rebecca Walton (2018, 241) call an "action-based approach," we introduce a brief history of countermemory and define and expound on this rhetorical construct while situating it as part of an interdisciplinary conversation about race, place, and public memory.

What Is Countermemory and How Does It Function?

The concept of countermemory is established and unpacked in this book to draw attention to dominant cultural narratives and the variety of ways in which they have been (and continue to be) disrupted. While we have used the term "liberatory countermemory" and even provided some examples, we want to clarify this concept and how it fits within a rhetorical framework. From the brief definition and examples we have already discussed and ones that we will examine in further chapters, readers may notice the variety of modes that countermemory can adopt, including books/articles, historic tours, monuments, memorials, songs, music videos, artwork, TV, movies, and maps. Conceptually, though, countermemory is rooted in rhetoric in that it highlights the ways we can make meaning and communicate ideas about identities, histories, and stories. As much as public memory is an inherently rhetorical pursuit, countermemory fits within the robust field of public memory research, both within rhetoric studies and in related fields. Thus, we position countermemory as an interdisciplinary project, like much of the public memory research that inspires and informs our scholarship.

Although countermemory is an expansive project in terms of its scope and interdisciplinarity, it is also focused and narrow in some aspects. In this book, we focus on race and racism and note the tensions between dominant white narratives and countermemory narratives that push back against these widely accepted cultural stories, what we might refer to as liberatory countermemories. Particularly, we examine Black, Latinx, and Indigenous countermemories in the United States. Since countermemory addresses how historically marginalized groups disrupt whiteness in public memory, there are many more stories that we could have included. However, we chose to focus on Black, Latinx, and Indigenous countermemories simply because the breadth and extent of violence, injustice, and racism is most pervasive and extreme within these communities (Gruenewald 2021, 6–7). Finally, our study is regionally focused in the US South (and Southwest, depending on how you define "the South" and underscoring that this region is not a monolith). We recognize that countermemory operates in other regions of the United States and abroad, but for our purposes, we seek to analyze and understand the ways in which the US South impacts countermemory and vice versa, especially because many sites and stories that promote dominant white narratives either originate in the South or refer to this region.

This book responds to the persistence of dominant cultural narratives in our nation's public memory and argues for the need for countermemories to disrupt and replace them. Public memory differs from history in key ways; as Pierre Nora (1989) writes, memory and history exist in "fundamental opposition" (8). As James Chase Sanchez (2020) explains it, where history studies the records, texts, and artifacts of any given social period, public memory is the way that a society chooses to remember its history, who and what it chooses to memorialize and glorify through storytelling, monuments, and public commemorations. As a result, public memory is subject to the demands of dominant narratives, such as what Gast's painting expresses about "American Progress." Gast's painting illustrates a constant narrative of white male advancement, which continues in spite of people of color's existence in our country. To advance that narrative, our nation has adopted a collective public memory that elides racialized individuals, events, and advancements. Dominant cultural narratives are transmitted in a variety of spaces and places, including historical monuments and memorials, heritage tourism sites, maps, and pop cultural sites. Among the American South's dominant narratives are the Lost Cause, which erases the memory of slavery and the colonization of Indigenous land while valorizing Confederate leaders. Only recently, since the beginning of the Black Lives Matter movement in 2013 and its resurgence in 2020, have many of Lost Cause monuments been removed. While these actions are commendable, without composing countermemories in their place, the act does not fully re/educate Americans about the histories that have been previously erased or forgotten. Removing monuments is the least that our country can do, and there is much more action needed to redress the injustices that have been inflicted on racialized peoples.

This book focuses on the various constructions of liberatory countermemory—their exigencies, how and why they form, where they form, and the reactions to their constructions. Ultimately, we contend that countermemory is a rhetorical construction that deserves as much attention—if not more—as public memory because these sites and artifacts are rhetorical not only in construction, appearance, and discourse but in the ways they often agitate and evoke negative reactions from hegemonic communities. Their very essence necessitates a response. We therefore focus on countermemory in different forms, be it plaques, memorials, museums, plantation tours, TV shows, music videos, and art installations, to further illustrate the ways the countermemories build communities and antagonists and often spill out into public and communal discourse. Overall, we argue that liberatory countermemory invites an emotional response and that we can further understand its impact through rhetorical analysis.

Four Components of Countermemory

Ultimately, this book seeks to remind the reader of the impact of stories of American exceptionalism and white supremacy—stories many in our nation believe and tell and stories that many people have contested. Therefore, we devote each chapter to exploring the various modes in which countermemory functions, from highlighting places and artifacts, to considering maps and map-making, and through pop culture. Toward that end, we focus on discourse and site analysis to study places and artifacts, as well as close reading, visual rhetoric, and material rhetoric. Given the recent efforts to incorporate enslaved narratives at heritage tourism sites, the growth in countermemory in entertainment via streaming shows like *Watchmen* and *Lawman: Bass Reeves*, and even the more expansive national conversation about the role of Confederate imagery and artifacts, the question is not *if* countermemory will continue to grow in our national imagination but *how*. How does countermemory differ from what we think about public memory? Where does countermemory exist, and how is it performed? How can countermemory be expressed in different media—be it statues, monuments, plaques, books, movies, songs, music videos, memes, and other artifacts? How does countermemory intersect with tourism industries? What is the relationship between identity, bigotry, and countermemory, or specifically race, racism, and countermemory? Why is race an important function that we should name in this work? These questions encompass the main themes of this book and help us explore the various rhetorical extensions and constructions of countermemory, while our multifaceted and layered analysis provides answers. While this text mostly composes arguments about liberatory countermemory, we believe those arguments are intrinsically tied into discourse about race and racism. Since slavery and racism are America's "original sin," we believe that liberatory countermemory disrupts normalized constructs of history and public memory that are distinctively tied to race. The two cannot be separated from one another. So, as we attempt to answer these questions, we will use liberatory countermemory as a lens to discuss race and race as a lens to discuss countermemory.

In the following chapters, we share our analysis and findings based on the questions that we have posed. Through our discourse and site analysis of countermemory places, along with our close reading and amplification of visual and material rhetorics to study other types of countermemory artifacts, we have found that countermemory runs contrary to most dominant white narratives, functions via a variety of modes of communication, and exists as a source of debate in many sociopolitical venues like school board meetings, political debates, and discussions around textbook creation. Before we consider these impacts, we want to unpack the five key components of countermemory, to more closely define the concept. These components substantiate countermemory as an area of study and an act of resistance. We want to note that while we briefly explain their definitions here, these principles are points of analysis or themes that appear in all our chapters and are the building blocks for our understanding of countermemory. Therefore, we view these principles as formations that we better expand and demonstrate throughout the rest of our book via implicit and explicit analysis.

First, liberatory countermemory opposes accepted views of history and memory by marking them as contested. Often, dominant or hegemonic narratives are disguised as "objectively true" or "historical facts." Liberatory countermemory endeavors to resist such narratives by questioning their veracity and presenting new narratives that completely oppose the dominant ones or complicate them. Thus, countermemory disrupts and deconstructs by either presenting a competing narrative based on the same evidence, augmenting the narrative already in place with additional information, or telling the story from the perspective of a marginalized group or person. Countermemory implicitly opposes accepted narratives but can also be more explicit in defying it as well. Take, for example, the hegemonic narratives communicated at the Alamo in San Antonio, Texas. When visitors listen to the audio tour or read the text on exhibits, monuments, or markers, they will hear a narrative that positions Anglo soldiers as heroic and Tejano and Mexican fighters as enemies. Likewise, there are no discussions of the role of slavery in the battle or how the Kickapoo, Comanche, Wichita, and Apache were violently removed from central Texas (Hernandez and O'Brien, 2024). In contrast, Brian Burrough, Chris Tomlinson, and Jason Stanford's (2021) *Forget the Alamo* presents a competing narrative, arguing that the reason the war was fought was to ensure that slavery would be preserved in the territory and future republic. Likewise, the entire #BlackLivesMatter campaign can be viewed as a form of countermemory, marked oftentimes by physical resistance but also constituted via even the name "Black Lives Matter." Historically, Black lives have not mattered in the United States. The phrase thus *repositions* Black lives in the future tense: Black lives should matter. The movement and the term challenge how white Americans have perceived Black deaths historically and in the present and contest all platitudes that say "all lives have always mattered," because they have not. Again, the phrase "Black Lives Matter," like the book *Forget the Alamo*, demonstrates how countermemory forms new narratives that run contrary to dominant cultural narratives that would argue "All Lives Matter" or that Mexican and Tejano voices were not significant in the Alamo battle. Countermemory looks beyond widely accepted narratives to uncover stories that have been erased or suppressed in the pursuit of white supremacy.

Second, liberatory countermemory attempts to bring to the public eye inequalities, tragedies, and injustices that are forgotten or erased. Running parallel to our first point, liberatory countermemory actively seeks to remember that which has been forgotten, misinterpreted, or co-opted because memorials function as memory aids for the public. Dominant public memory functions in such a way that the stories of white men are valorized and accepted as mainstream, even if historical records contest these honorifics. For example, elementary history teaches that Christopher Columbus was a brave explorer who sought to bring Christianity to the West Indies. Readers of this book may find such a narrative humorous at best and offensive at worst; primary documents, like Columbus's own diary, would disagree with such a narrative. Yet many right-leaning Americans would accept this story as inherently true and welcome it as part of their value system. Several GOP leaders tweeted in support of Columbus in 2022 (Polus 2022). Representative Elise Stefanik (R-NY) condemned any attempt to refocus the day on Indigenous people: "I am proud to stand up against the Far Left woke mob attempting to cancel history! #SaveColumbusDay" (@elisestefanik 2022). In contrast to narratives that still attempt to portray Columbus as someone who "dreamed big" and "discovered the Americas" are more recent movements toward celebrating Indigenous Peoples Day (Polus 2022). Indigenous Peoples Day demonstrates this important component of countermemory—namely the way countermemory brings to attention the inequalities, tragedies, and injustices that have been forgotten or erased. On that same day, Senator Tammy Duckworth (D-IL) demonstrates this rhetorical movement with her tweet: "On #IndigenousPeoplesDay, let us pause to remember the exploitation and genocide of Native and Indigenous communities borne out of our nation's 'discovery'" (@SenDuckworth 2022). A few communities have even altered entire memory landscapes by reckoning with Columbus's history. For instance, in

Newark, New Jersey, the city took down its Columbus statue after incidents of 2020 vandalism and eventually replaced it with a statue of Harriet Tubman in 2023 (Franklin 2023).

Some other examples of this function of countermemory can be located in recent years in heritage tourism sites like plantation homes and urban slavery homes. At Whitney Plantation in Louisiana, countermemory is enacted by focusing on the lived experiences of enslaved individuals instead of the opulent lifestyle of the owners of the enslaved. Likewise, visitors are educated about the memory of enslaved individuals, including their names, family histories, and skills. Rather than spending most of the tour in the "big house," a tour at Whitney ends with a tour of the home after instructing visitors about the implications of the luxurious home being a direct result of human trafficking and enslavement.

Third, liberatory countermemory links the past and present by showing how our violent histories and present injustices are interrelated. Since many white Americans tend to distance themselves from events or individuals that remind them of our country's racism and settler-colonialism, liberatory countermemory creates a continuous narrative that forms connections between past events and current concerns. For example, consider the National Memorial for Peace and Justice (NMPJ), which depicts the United States' legacy of lynching. To create one continuous narrative about violence toward Black Americans, the NMPJ opens with sculptures of enslaved individuals, progresses through the indoor section that names the individuals who were lynched, and leads back to an outdoor area with another sculpture of Black men with their hands up. The movement through the memorial thus takes the visitor on a chronological journey, one that materially and physically links the country's history of slavery with its present-day concerns of violence against and imprisonment of Black men. Such connections between the past and the present are found in most countermemory artifacts and sites. At the Owens-Thomas House and Slave Quarters in Savannah, Georgia, historical interpreters also make overt connections between the past and the present. Many heritage tourism sites tend to portray the home and its inhabitants as if they are fictional characters in an Old South drama, but Owens-Thomas historical interpreters trace themes like Black resistance or systemic injustice in their tours. While they still highlight aspects of the home and its inhabitants, historical interpreters are careful to tie together the issues of the past to contemporary events and discussions (Browning-Mullis 2022). As a result, visitors are compelled to grapple with issues of racism, rather than viewing slavery as something that occurred hundreds of years ago with no impacts on our current sociopolitical climate. Thus, we find that countermemory is characterized by finding links between past and current events, with a call to action to visitors who interact with these sites and artifacts.

Fourth, due to its confrontational nature, liberatory countermemory often elicits challenges or violent reactions by people who choose not to accept these memories as history. Most examples of countermemory do not exist as peaceful refutations of accepted history because they are confrontational by nature. Those who represent hegemonic ideas of history must confront, refute, and attack them as a means of keeping their own views of history and ideologies intact. Nowhere are these attacks more evident than in grade schools. After the murder of George Floyd in June 2020, there was a window in time when some white Americans were more open to conversations about systemic racism. Thus, even the assertion of systemic racism is an act of countermemory. In response to more open conversations about systemic racism in the summer of 2020, Republican politicians across the country created new bills (some of which have been written into law since then) to prevent teachers from discussing racism as a current problem in the United States. In Texas, for example, teachers must present "both sides" of historical events like slavery and are encouraged to not discuss current events (Texas House Bill 3979). Critical race theory (CRT) has become the latest issue in conservative culture wars, and in many right-wing circles, any discussion of racism is deemed "CRT" and not to be included in the grade school curriculum. In mid-2020, for instance, Republican senator Tom Cotton of Arkansas attempted to pass a bill that would ban schools from using *The 1619 Project* in the classroom (Armus 2020). Cotton argued the project, which was vetted by many historians but is still controversial, "cannot get the facts right." His attack on a historical project illustrates how hegemonic actors often react when countermemory disagrees with their feelings and ideologies.

Fifth, liberatory countermemory can be defined by its absences and presences, by naming what is and is not physically located at specific sites of memory. Most sites in this book are named and draw rhetorical interest via their physical properties: the human-made design of memorials, statues, and monuments and the discursive text of place markers. Where humans design and create memoryscapes, rhetorical value can be easily assigned. However, countermemories can also be defined by their absences too. Take, for instance, the lynching of James Byrd Jr. in Jasper, Texas, in 1998. Byrd's death by the hands of three white supremacists made national news, and President Obama even signed a hate prevention act in his honor in 2009. One might assume that such a publicly staged death would force the people of Jasper to create memories in Byrd's honor. But they did not. Rather, they named a playground for him on the outskirts of town. We will discuss this example in more detail in chapter 4, on our countermemory tour, but it is important to name here that the lack of memory sites dedicated to Byrd says as much about what Jasper values as a true memorial dedicated to him might. If the community is only willing to name a park after him—with no mention of what happened to him in 1999—then what are they saying about how they value Byrd? Do they align themselves as viewing him as a victim of a heinous, white supremacist murder or do their values lead them to just want to forget him and his death? The absences of countermemory hold as much rhetorical power as the presences.

These five components illustrate the key pillars in building a texture of liberatory countermemory, one that exists outside of abstract ideologies and lives in everyday communities and spaces around the United States. The rest of the book expands on these components and provides context while describing them via sites, artifacts, and pop culture.

However, it is important to note here why are specifically referring to "liberatory" countermemories and not just countermemory more broadly. Since the United States public often remembers history and historical figures from a hegemonic perspective, in which those in power are the ones writing and prescribing which histories should be remembered, most countermemories, by definition, would be liberatory. They exist in public spheres in order to challenge these hegemonic forces and to give people with less power a space to create their own memories. We see this in many of the racialized public memories we will discuss in this book.

Still, there are acts of countermemory that would not fit under this liberatory definition. For instance, compare the acts of vandalism against the Christopher Columbus statue in Boston, in which protestors beheaded the historical figure (Buell 2020), with the vandalism committed against the plaque dedicated to the site where Emmett Till's body was found, which people have routinely riddled with bullet holes (Tell 2019). Both vandalisms could be described as acts of countermemory since they challenge values being displayed in public forums. Yet, there is an inherent difference in the power structures described by these acts. With the Columbus memorial, the beheading, while perhaps viewed as crass and potentially "violent" (symbolically speaking) by the public, disputes the normalized history of Columbus as the "founder" of the United States. The historical monuments to Columbus downplay the genocidal and errant ideologies central to his exploration and "discoveries." The beheading act, then, can be interpreted as a rewriting of history in which protestors challenge Columbus's importance, nondiscursively stating that we no longer need to respect Columbus as a "pioneer" or a "discoverer." It liberates this public memory from an inherently white, Eurocentric perspective that downplays the history of Native Americans, colonialism, and genocide.

The bullet holes imprinted in the Till historical marker do not fit into the same type of countermemory narrative as the Columbus statute beheading. In this case, the bullet holes must be interpreted as either protestors challenging the importance of Till as a historical figure or as a symbolic threat against Black people. Upon the sign being vandalized, Anthea Hartig, the director of the National Museum of American History, claimed, "The history of racial violence is often erased and highly contested in the battle to define American memory, and this vandalized sign demonstrates the ramifications of ongoing efforts of remembrance and social justice. Racism does not only reside in the past; it inhabits our lived reality" ("Smithsonian to Display Emmett Till Historical Marker" 2021). The challenges of those carrying out the vandalism run counter to the acceptance of Till as a historical figure and as a victim of racist violence in mid-twentieth-century Mississippi. By every definition of countermemory, these presumably white individuals attempted to "counter" an accepted history of racism in the South and Till's significance; their act literally attempts to replace or erase him. Yet, even compared to the Columbus activism and in regard to hegemony and power, this act could not be perceived as liberatory. Rather, it beckons to the racism and white pride in the era preceding the civil rights movement, when figures like Till could be murdered and pulled from the annals of history. The power struggle embedded within the bullet holes neither calls for racial equity and equality nor opposes a top-down model of history. It promotes white supremacy. It calls for us to go back to a time in history when racial violence was accepted as the norm.

We provide these detailed examples to emphasize that the focus of this book is on liberatory countermemories, highlighting moments when (often racialized) actors contest hegemonic, white, and Eurocentric views of history. While the study of nonliberatory countermemories—or what we might call countermemory *ad antiquitatem* (Latin for "for antiquity") since these memories typically call for us to go back to an antiquated time in the past when racism, homophobia, and prejudices were accepted—is a fruitful avenue of exploration, it is not our focus. Future texts should be dedicated to such research.

Our Approach to Studying Countermemory

Our argument in this study is based on an interdisciplinary analysis of sites and artifacts of countermemory focusing on visual material rhetorics, space/place studies, and public memory combining methods and methodologies from rhetoric, cultural geography, and tourism studies. The choice to draw from interdisciplinary scholarship is threefold. First, we find that while rhetoric and writing studies have explored various aspects of public memory, race, and place, there is room for a deeper examination of the intersection of these three areas; thus, it is at this junction that we position countermemory: where research and praxis of public memory, race, and place are found. Second, scholars in cultural geography (including the subfield of Black feminist geography) have engaged in several decades of research pertaining to issues of race and place. In fact, it is cultural geographer Stephen Legg from whom we borrow the term "countermemory" and consider its meaning for rhetorical studies. Thus, we locate cultural geography and related fields within our study of rhetorical countermemory and argue that they provide greater granularity to our arguments and examinations. Third, it is important to us to cite women and people of color in this project, which is in its nature as a project that pushes back against hegemony. Following the practices of scholars like Sara Ahmed, Rebecca Walton, Kristen Moore, and Natasha Jones, and Richard Delgado (1984) and Jean Stefancic, we, too, seek to highlight nonmainstream scholarship and practices. We employ methods and methodologies that reflect an overarching goal to be inclusive. As a practice, countermemory is a rhetoric of resistance; thus, we feel that our methodologies should also demonstrate that same commitment to scholarly resistance in terms of who we cite. While we draw from a wide range of interdisciplinary scholarship in rhetoric studies, cultural geography, history, and cultural rhetorics, we intentionally cite Black scholars and other scholars of color because their voices are invaluable to our arguments. We recognize the systemic racism that is pervasive within academia, and our citational choices are one way to attempt to create a more equitable space.

Countermemory is a book about race/racism, place, and public memory; thus, our methodologies mirror these themes. Large portions of this book study sites and objects, so we employ a three-pronged approach. We examine memorials, monuments, markers, or tours from a perspective of visual material rhetorics, space/place, and public memory. What that means is that we analyze examples of countermemory by considering their physical characteristics and the rhetorical impact in the larger psychogeographic space–all within the already existing public memory framework. Recognizing that countermemory is a disruptive practice, we consider how sites of countermemory enact a critical spatial perspective.

Visual Material Rhetorics

First, we draw from an interdisciplinary approach to visual material rhetorics for our site-based analysis and our study of artifacts like memorials or countermaps. We keep in mind the role of materiality, new materialism, and visual-material rhetorics as theoretical concepts that inform the ways in which we examine and understand sites and artifacts of countermemory. For example, the site-based analysis of Whitney Plantation in Louisiana contemplates "the interplay between textual, visual, and material ways of knowing" (Propen 2012, 4). However, our use of these theories is cautious and self-reflexive, especially in light of the appropriation of Indigenous ways of knowing by white settler scholars. Over the last decade, many scholars in the field of rhetoric and composition have embarked on theories and practices of object-oriented ontologies, posthumanism, new materialism, and affect studies. As part of the "material turn," scholars in rhetoric and composition tend to highlight the work of the same group of thinkers and fail to give equal textual space to the many Indigenous researchers who conceived these theories long before Heidegger and Latour. As a field, we have, in the words of Sara Ahmed (2020) and Zoe Todd (2016, 11), "whitened up to lighten up."

We recognize our positionality as non-Indigenous scholars (O'Brien identifies as white settler and Sanchez as Latinx) and also note that Western (European and white American) constructions of object-oriented ontologies, posthumanism, new materialism, and affect studies tend to erase Indigenous ways of knowing (Sundberg 2013, 35). Likewise, since countermemory is rooted in resisting dominant cultural narratives, it would be hypocritical and unethical to engage in conversations about materiality without highlighting the work of Indigenous scholarship. However, we also want to point out that this project does not illustrate decolonial methodology. As Cana Uluak Itchuaqiyaq and Breeanne Matheson (2021, 9) establish, the work of decolonial methodologies is distinct from the more generalized work of social justice scholarship and necessitates overt partnerships with Indigenous communities for the betterment of those communities. Rather, we seek to engage with Indigenous frameworks of materiality in our study of countermemory to provide a more robust understanding of sites and artifacts. Thus, we find that the work of countermemory is not just theoretical; it is material. In this chapter, we seek to incorporate what Dwayne Donald (2009) calls "ethical relationality," which is "an ecological understanding of human relationality that does not deny difference, but rather seeks to more deeply understand how our different histories and experiences position us in relation to each other" (6). As we examine how materiality, new materialism, and visual-material rhetorics inform our site-based analysis, we do not "overlook or invisibilize the [. . .] historical, cultural, and social contexts" that surround these theories and practices (Donald 2009, 6).

We foreground materiality because each site or artifact of countermemory is inherently rhetorical. While crafted by humans, the sites persuade and impact the surrounding space. This spatialized and embodied impact reflects the comprehensive ontology of Indigenous ways of knowing (see Kimmerer 2013; TallBear 2015), or as it is designated in rhetoric and composition, ambience (see Rickert 2013) or rhetorical ecologies (see Edbauer 2009). We want to emphasize the rhetoricity of these sites or artifacts and the impact of each in the surrounding psychogeographic space. In our site analysis, whether we are highlighting the rhetorical impact of hanging steel columns with the names of individuals who were hanged, a memorial with a Black family placed in the center of Savannah's tourism spaces (steps from where ships of the enslaved were docked), or a spatialized conflict over the placement of a historical marker text, we situate these objects/artifacts as "agential beings engaged in social relations that profoundly shape human lives" (TallBear 2015, 234). As TallBear writes, these nonhuman objects and sites engage in a social relationship with the surrounding area(s) and people. Likewise, as Jenny Edbauer (2009) contends, "The rhetorical situation is part of what we might call . . . an ongoing social flux. Situation bleeds into the concatenation of public interaction. Public interactions bleed into wider social processes. The elements of rhetorical situation simply bleed" (8–9). For example, when in 2002 Savannah erected the city's first monument commemorating Black history, the effects extended far beyond the physical space into the historic community's identity and the heritage tourism industry at large. The ongoing social flux includes the eleven-year battle to get the monument approved by government officials and local situations, but it also includes the way the monument has shifted the tourism industry in Savannah, which over the last twenty years has slowly begun to discuss the city's relationship with slavery and its Black community.

We often view relationships between objects/sites and the surrounding psychogeographic spaces as assemblages. Scholarship across philosophy, rhetoric and writing studies, and cultural geography identify the term "assemblage" as disparate and collective groupings (Braidotti 2019; Deleuze and Guattari 1987; Yancey and McElroy 2017; Beck 2015; Bennett 2010). Elsewhere, O'Brien (2020) considers assemblage as a relationship between human bodies and sites of memory and argues that our bodies become a part of public memory. In her work, Rosi Braidotti (2019) insists that the posthuman "can be put to the collective task of constructing new subjects of knowledge, through immanent assemblages or transversal alliances between multiple actors" (6). Not only do assemblages represent a material, embodied relationship between objects and humans but they constitute new forms of knowledge. In the case of Whitney Plantation, there are various configurations of assemblage, but one April noted in particular during her visit was the tourists and the memorial wall that lists the names of the enslaved who labored there. The memorial is composed of a glossy black granite material—when visitors stand in front of these long walls, they can see their own reflection like a palimpsest together with the names. The granite wall, a nonhuman feature, contributes to the rhetorical impact and affect of the memorial simply because of its glossy appearance. Assemblage theories inform our site analyses because, as Zoe Todd (2016) writes, these sites/objects engage are a part of a larger "cosmolog[y] that enmesh people into complex relationships between themselves and all relations" (6). Whether visitors realize it or not, they become enmeshed with/in the memorial and are compelled to question their relationship and/or complicity with slavery in the United States.

As we position sites and objects of countermemory within an assemblage of rhetorical impact, by extension, we consider the vitality of these things or spaces that are not alive. In her research about the Dakota pipeline, TallBear (2015) notes that the pipeline does not have blood or DNA or a "cellular vibrancy."

Yet, she asserts that the stone "is spoken of as a relative" (233). Robin Kimmerer (2013) speaks of a similar relationship in *Braiding Sweetgrass*, where she sees the hand of Skywoman, the Iroquois mother goddess, in the honeyed scent of sweetgrass (12). From TallBear's and Kimmerer's research, we apply vitality to inanimate objects like a historical marker text in Slocum, Texas, or to the clay sculptures of enslaved children at Whitney Plantation. These objects are not alive, yet they contain an "energetic vitality," a "thing-power [where] inanimate things [. . .] animate [and] act to produce effects dramatic and subtle" (Bennett 2010, 5, 6).

To understand countermemory sites and artifacts, we also turn to visual-material rhetorics, which focuses on the interplay between the visual and textual (Propen 2012, xvi). Propen argues for "a visual rhetoric that more expressly accounts not only for a rhetorical artifact's material and spatial components but also for its subsequent impact on the body" (3). We, too, seek to bring the body into our site analysis, as seen earlier in how we contend that assemblage should be viewed as an embodied theory, but also in how we position the impact of these sites and artifacts on the body. In her book *Locating Visual-Material Rhetorics*, Propen also performs a site analysis of the Lowell Mills in Boston and finds that the visual-material approach allows her to examine both the spatial layout of the park as well as its various structures, buildings, and memorials. In doing so, Propen extends an argument that these structures and their layout contribute to a greater sense of empathy for the young women who labored in these mills in the nineteenth century (49). Likewise, applying visual-material rhetorics to our site analyses helps foster a deeper understanding of the historical underpinnings in each site, as well as how this knowledge interplays with the lived experience of those being remembered and those visiting these sites. Such a perspective has the potential to enact further change as countermemory circulates in the public sphere. Furthermore, visual-material rhetorics is also tied to how we view and interpret space and place as rhetorical constructs, as Propen (2012) writes: "I have often understood visual and material artifacts largely through both a rhetorical and a geographical lens–as discursive objects that facilitate spatial understanding, are situated in time and space, and much important claims to knowledge" (xxv). As we discuss and analyze the material and textual features of these sites, incorporating a theory of space and place allows us to consider the relationship to the land, as well as how geography and the use of space informs and persuades.

Space/Place as Rhetorical

The rhetoricity of space and place has been a particularly prolific area of study in rhetoric and writing studies, especially over the last twenty years. When we write that space/place is rhetorical, we follow a long line of scholars in rhetoric and writing who have established a link between rhetoric studies and geography (Blair 1999; Boyle and Rice 2018; Dickinson, Ott, and Aoki 2006; Gruenwald 2021; Monroe 2021; Reynolds 2004). Nedra Reynolds (2004) describes the role of place and memory in rhetoric: "Memory and place, location and argument, walking and learning, are vitally and dramatically linked in our personal histories and personal geographies. Places evoke powerful human emotions because they become layered, like sediment or a palimpsest, with histories and stories and memories" (2). Likewise, Casey Boyle and Jenny Rice (2018) write in their edited collection, *Inventing Place*, a collection of essays about place and Texas, that "as our own bodies and senses move through space, our encounters with those spaces form a kind of embodied knowledge and valuation of those spaces" (2). These arguments about space and place are foundational; yet in this book, we seek to take the path that Reynolds does in hers: we focus on how cultural geographers theorize space and place, particularly those who study the role of race, racism, indigeneity, and settler colonialism as it is exemplified in space and place.

The study of space and place has long been a site of critical theory in cultural geography. What cultural geographers call a critical spatial perspective is, above all, a call to consider how space and spatialization affects human beings. For the purpose of providing a framework for a site analysis of countermemory, these theories of critical spatial perspectives are most relevant to our work. We are most interested in the scholarship in cultural geography (and in rhetoric and writing studies) that attends to concerns of what Edward Soja (2010, 4) calls "spatial justice" and David Sibley (1995) calls "geographies of exclusion" (ix). These scholars, along with others, examine space and place alongside issues of race and racism and settler colonialism. We choose to focus on this area of space and place studies because a site analysis of countermemory requires a critical eye that views space as "the product of interrelations" of power and agency (Massey 2005, 9). There is nothing neutral or unbiased about space and place, and this knowledge is what makes sites of countermemory so powerful and effective. Natchee Blu Barnd (2017) writes, "Any dominant form of space or spatiality stands as, and is, power, as it structures particular values about, views of, and practices within the world and reinforces these structures by shaping encounters to match that world" (13). Sites like the NMPJ, which are located within traditional Old South memoryscapes in Montgomery, Alabama, are particularly compelling as they begin to change the values and views about lynching, slavery, and structural racism within unfriendly spaces. Similarly, in the sites we highlight in this book, we focus on the spatiality of the sites as well as the way the space invokes power and agency across "real and imagined" spaces and places (Soja 1996, 6). These real and imagined spaces include the material sites and surrounding areas as well as the impact of these sites on metaphysical registers.

The impact of these geographies extends far beyond the material world into the psyche of the community and beyond, especially as these sites form part of local and national tourism industries.

While a theory of spatial justice is key to understanding the purpose and significance of countermemory sites, we need to first begin with a theory of spatialized difference. The fact that spatialized difference exists is why we need a theory of spatial justice. In the introduction to his book *Geographies of Difference*, David Sibley (1995) writes, "The human landscape can be read as a landscape of exclusion" (ix). In his book, Sibley focuses on what he calls "opaque instances of exclusion," which are the kinds of spatialized exclusion that have become normalized by mainstream culture (ix). A way to understand how exclusion operates is to study who places are for, whom they exclude, and how the system of exclusion is enforced (x). Sociospatial exclusion is a way to separate groups of people, a system generally based on race and racism, but it is also observable via class, education, gender, sexuality, and ableness (xvi). It is when we overlay theories of difference atop the dominant structure of remembrance in our country that we can understand the relationship between difference and countermemory. When applied to public memory, sociospatial exclusion takes on a variety of positions. For example, the majority of tours of plantations either ignore, misrepresent, or downplay the role of slavery (Hanna et al. 2019; Poirot and Watson 2015; O'Brien 2020b; McKittrick 2011). Out of the over 16,000 historical markers in Texas, there are only 142 that address multiply marginalized communities and many of these examples do so in a way that is harmful to these communities (O'Brien 2021, 8). Texas has arguably the most robust historical marker program in the country, and it was not until 2006 that the Texas Historical Commission (THC) recognized that countermemory needed to be reflected within the current memory system in place. Barnd (2017) explains that "producing space is both a conceptual and material process" that shapes the way we see and engage with it, and these examples of the plantation tours and the Texas commission demonstrate how sociospatial inclusion has been enacted in public memory sites that communicate our nation's history to the general public (22). From these examples, we argue that sites of countermemory are needed precisely because sociospatial exclusion dominates many memoryscapes in the United States. Space is used to exclude groups of people and to confirm a single story about American history.

It is because sociospatial exclusion continues to exist, both in terms of how and where multiple marginalized and underrepresented people are allowed to live and work and in how their memory is withheld from public spaces and memory, that spatial justice enters into the discussion. Spatial justice is the "geography of social justice" (Soja 2010, 4), and it is characterized by using spaces and places to redress social injustices. As Soja (1996) argues, "Allowing the 'subaltern' to speak, to assert an-Other voice, pushes the discourses on to a different plane and into a recreative space of radical openness where both development and social justice can be revisioned together, along with their histories and geographies" (126). Countermemory is characterized by asserting "an-Other voice," and these voices typically have been dismissed, erased, or minimized by dominant cultural narratives. Another way of viewing spatial justice and "an-Other voice" is via the scholarship of Indigenous geographies, which announce "we [Native individuals] are still here" (Barnd 2017, 1). Indigenous geographies illustrate "how mundane practices of geographic imagining play a pivotal role in the processes of colonization and decolonization, with both processes being understood as ongoing, contemporary projects rather than concluded, historic ones" (78). In her analysis of Native American museums in the United States, Lisa King (2017) argues that there is not a single way for Native individuals to represent themselves in these spaces; rather, each considers the role of audience and individual goals. King's work, along with Barnd's and others', promotes spatial justice by reminding white settlers that issues of justice are not just historical, they are current. Thus, when sites of countermemory combat dominant narratives by a strategic and intentional use of space, discourses can move toward justice.

Public Memory

In the field of rhetoric, public memory studies can be traced back to the early 1990s. While the study of memory has been a cornerstone in the field since Quintilian and Cicero discussed the *memoriae* and mnemonics, the idea of public memory—or memory substantiated in public spaces (like memorials, monuments, and local folklore) that constructs, cultivates, and shapes individuals and collectives—is a newer area of study. In the 1990s, articles in the field focused on postmodernity and the memory of war (Blair, Jeppeson, and Pucci 1991); public memory as a rhetorical method (Browne 1995); public and private grief of national tragedies (Jorgensen-Earp and Lanzilotti 1998); and the politics of memory (Browne 1999). These articles established public memory as a rhetorical subject that builds and reflects communities and illustrates the meaning-making that occurs from memories that are difficult to process.

The 2000s led to expanding the rhetoric of public memory from an interdisciplinary perspective to one that integrated analysis on museums as an important public memory-making endeavor as well. Kendall Phillips published his edited collection *Framing Public Memory*, in 2004 and weaved the differences between public, national, and cultural memory through different chapters. Phillips's text centered public memory studies as a uniquely rhetorical subject, creating an exigence for other scholars to respond. Over the next few years, other texts focused on subfields of public memory studies were published, including issues with forgetting (Vivian 2010), race and ethnicity (Reyes 2010), and museums (Dickinson, Blair, and Ott 2010). These texts also correspond with a movement over the last few decades in rhetoric studies to consider the rhetoricity of memory sites and to argue for a distinct link between rhetoric and memory studies. All of these texts touch on the relationship between space/place and public memory to a degree, but more recent scholars have further intertwined public memory with space/place, as seen in Casey Boyle and Jenny Rice's edited collection, *Inventing Place* (2018); Samantha Senda-Cook, Michael Middleton, and Danielle Endres's "Rhetorical Cartographies: (Counter)Mapping Urban Spaces" (2018); Tim Gruenewald's *Curating America's Painful Past* (2021); and Stephen Monroe's *Heritage and Hate* (2021). The field of public memory studies continues to grow.

Yet, while public memory studies and space/place studies have further developed public memory as rhetorical, neither have considered countermemory, a term cultural geographer Legg employs extensively. Conceptually, Legg connects countermemory to Walter Benjamin's work, but for the actual term, "sites of countermemory," he credits Michel Foucault as well as Pierre Nora, a French historian. According to Legg (2005), "sites of counter-memory mark times and places in which people have refused to forget. They can rebut the memory schema of a dominant class, caste, race, or nation, providing an alternative form of remembering and identity" (181). Following Walter Benjamin's warning about historicism, Legg asserts that the way public memory is presented historically does not actually recognize the overlooked stories of marginalized individuals and events. For Legg, a more accurate representation of history comes from the idea of melancholia in Benjamin's "On the Concept of History" (1940; 2006). Because of the flawed way that we remember history, Benjamin recommends that we maintain an active, evolving, and melancholic attitude toward the past. When we adopt a mournful posture toward history, it "generates sites for memory and history, for the rewriting of the past as well as the reimagining of the future" (Eng and Kazanjian 2003, 1). The focus of Legg's research is how certain memories are repressed or forgotten in Delhi, a similar pattern that we trace in the American South with regards to African American, Indigenous, and Chicanx stories. As he analyzes various contested spaces and places in Delhi, he (2005) applies the term "sites of counter-memory": "This phrase combines the work of Foucault with French historian Pierre Nora. Nora coined the phrase *lieux de mémoire* (sites, places, or realms of memory) to represent the ways people came to identify with the nation" (183). As such, sites of countermemory are characterized by a challenging—even a disruption—of dominant historical narratives. These sites can also be material, digital, metaphysical, or symbolic.

Also taking up countermemory, cultural geographer Derek Alderman examines the African American Monument in Savannah, Georgia, and focuses on the complex relationship between contested public memory and Savannah's

African American community. He describes the lengthy battle that teacher and activist Abigail Jordan fought to get the monument approved, the debate over the monument's text (taken from Maya Angelou's writing), and the conflict with local leaders and community members over all aspects of the monument (its placement, the text, and its purpose). Alderman (2010) argues that the monument represents a site of countermemory, and, drawing from Legg, also establishes how these sites function to remember the forgotten or suppressed stories: "The construction of counter-memory can be highly contentious because of the political stakes involved and the inherent difficulty of recovering long repressed (and suppressed) memories and identities" (90–91). In spite of the opposition, countermemory still is able to form, whether in response to historical events or current conversations that highlight injustices.

The Formation of Countermemory

We argue that one reason countermemory forms is in response to historical and contemporary violence toward Black, Indigenous, and People of Color (BIPOC). As violence has increased, countermemory has increased as well and has taken the form of various efforts, including acts of resistance. While #Resist and #BlackLivesMatter encompass a wide range of ideological stances, including acts of civil disobedience, relief efforts for immigrants, and supporting marginalized communities, the concept of resistance is also tied to place, race, and public memory. James Chase Sanchez and Kristen Moore (2015) argue that acts of resistance have "an affective ripple effect" and that "the rhetorical work of public memory is such that the resistant act will not be erased" (5). In this case, countermemory takes the form of tagging of and/or forceful community-led removal of Confederate monuments. Some other examples include the removal of Silent Sam (a Confederate monument on the University of North Carolina Chapel Hill's campus); three monuments on the University of Texas's Austin campus; a Confederate monument in Birmingham, Alabama; two statues in Raleigh, North Carolina; and many others around the country (Bidgood et al. 2017).

These acts of removal, whether done quietly with little fanfare (as with the monuments on the University of Texas's campus) or by force by protestors, reflect the turn in popular opinion since white supremacists took to the national stage in the streets of Charlottesville, Virginia. Scholars have long demonstrated multiple key problems with public memory in the United States, particularly as it is expressed in historical memorials, monuments, and markers. There are close to one thousand Confederate memorials, markers, and monuments funded by the United Daughters of the Confederacy (UDC). In fact, no organization has been more effective in crafting Southern identity more than the UDC. Formed after the Civil War, the UDC wanted to create a southern identity that people could be proud of, especially when the American South was at a low point, economically and socially. They wanted to make sure that Confederate leaders were valorized, so in the forty-year span between 1880–1920, hundreds of memorials were erected in the South to commemorate Confederate leaders. The UDC was a proponent of a new ideology that argued 1) the Confederate fight was heroic, 2) enslaved people were happy, and 3) slavery was not the root cause of the war (Lowndes 2017). The UDC infiltrated public discourse through the creation of a shared southern identity via memorials and markers, as well as through textbooks for children (Loewen 1999). They set up rigid guidelines that referred back to the three tenets, and history textbooks had to adhere to them. The textbook writers were frequently Confederate soldiers as well. These textbooks were a part of the history classroom in the South as late as the 1970s.

As can be seen, memorials, monuments, and even history books do not represent history accurately. As James Loewen (1999) writes, "Most historic sites do not just tell stories about the past; they also tell visitors what to think about the stories they tell" (8). Furthermore, Loewen cites hundreds of examples around the country of historical sites that tell outright lies or shade information in tendentious ways. Similarly, the textbooks used by many schools omit or reframe issues like colonialism and slavery—a trend the UDC also had a hand in through the early 1980s (Lowndes 2017). The United States suffers from selective amnesia when it comes to remembering all aspects of its history, including its treatment of people of color, and many memorials, historic markers, and historical societies present a sanitized version of the past. As a result, "America has ended up with a landscape of denial" (Loewen 1999, 5). While this information is not new to scholars who study public memory with a critical eye, it is new to the general public—especially over the last decade, which is why we see more conversations about who should be memorialized and what we should do with these Confederate monuments if they are not displayed publicly. And these conversations have opened a space for countermemory to form. For instance, the THC's Undertold Markers Program is an example of countermemory occurring at the state level. The Undertold Markers Program was created to tell the stories that are not currently circulating in Texas's public memory. In other words, these markers inform the public of individuals, events, and sites that have been historically marginalized—because of Texas's geospatial location, this includes Chicanx, Mexican American, Black, and various Indigenous memories ("Undertold Markers," n.d.).

Expansion of Countermemory

While dominant cultural narratives have experienced periods of disruption, the last couple of decades have seen the most vibrant and noticeable upsurge in countermemory in the history of the United States. We have already mentioned social media activism that has increased in response to the continued murder of unarmed Black men—especially since Trayvon Martin's shooting in 2012. Since that time, the Marshall Project, "a nonpartisan, nonprofit news organization that seeks to create and sustain a sense of national urgency about the U.S. criminal justice system," has documented cases of violence against unarmed people of color, as well as other sites of injustice including immigration, mental health, and more generalized issues of racism ("Mission Statement," n.d.). The Marshall Project, along with many other endeavors, illustrates digital countermemory, standing alongside material sites of countermemory, like Whitney Plantation in Wallace, Louisiana. These digital sites are interdisciplinary, community-engaged projects that diffuse stories of people of color in direct opposition to whitesplained historical accounts.

In addition to digital countermemory, we can see an indicator of an increase in countermemory within the heritage tourism industry in the American South. In general, though, historical tourism in the region focuses on the wealthy white owners of the enslaved and their opulent lives and either ignores, minimizes, or lies about the experiences of the Black individuals who were enslaved at these sites. As Kristan Poirot and Shevaun Watson (2015) establish in their study of Charleston, South Carolina's, historical tourism industry, many of these sites actually serve to "reanimate white supremacy" through the performance of tours (93). April O'Brien and James Chase Sanchez (2021) also describe a plantation tour at Woodburn in western South Carolina where the docent not only focuses on the owners of the enslaved also attempts to downplay the daily reality and function of slavery at this house. Likewise, scholarship in cultural geography has analyzed various aspects of heritage tourism, including a study that uses narrative mapping to visualize how the history of slavery is incorporated into plantation tours (Hanna et al. 2019), another that analyzes the sequencing of narratives told at historical sites (Azaryahu and Foote 2008), and a yet another that explores the relationship between Black diasporic communities and plantations (McKittrick 2011). In a study that examines historical markers, monuments, historic homes, forts, and ships, sociologist and historian James Loewen (1999) uncovers overt racism in the way these artifacts and sites glorify the white historical figure, as well as providing outright lies or tendentiously shaded information (8). In short, there is ample scholarship that demonstrates the problematic portrayal of public memory and history. Yet, one of our aims in this book is to highlight sites of countermemory—either sites that have been revamped like Thomas Jefferson's Monticello home or new sites of countermemory that have been created, like Whitney Plantation, which reopened in 2014 as a museum.

Starting in the mid-2010s, tourism sites in the American South began a slow (and contested) revision to include a franker discussion of slavery, an evolution that some have argued is due to the #BlackLivesMatter movement (Mzezewa 2019). In Savannah, Georgia, the Owens-Thomas House added "and

Slave Quarters" to its official name in 2018, and the tour at this site now makes the connection between the Owens-Thomas wealth and the labor of the enslaved individuals who worked there. Likewise, in 2018, Monticello opened a new exhibit that conveys the fact that Jefferson had sexual intercourse (of debatable consentuality) with a woman he enslaved, Sally Hemings—a fact that has been purposely ignored by the tours until recently (Stockman 2018). The exhibit displays Hemings's living quarters, which was previously used as the men's restroom but now depicts oral histories of the descendants of enslaved people. Monticello is also phasing out its "house tour," which is generally the focus of most plantation tours, a focus that serves to elevate the significance of the white slave owners' history and erase the enslaved individuals (Stockman 2018). In Charleston, South Carolina, the McLeod Plantation has made dramatic changes to its tours, which include self-led and traditional tours, to fully incorporate a narrative that does not treat the enslaved as a footnote to the home's existence. During April's 2018 tour of McLeod, she noted the embodied and material changes on the tour: the enslaved people have names and their labor is noted throughout the grounds and property. From the first step in the welcome center, it was clear that the tour problematized the economic disparity that continues to this day as a result of slavery (O'Brien 2019, 141). More overt examples of countermemory include the erection of the NMPJ in Montgomery, Alabama, in memory of those who were lynched in the United States, and Whitney Plantation.

Similarly, in the early twenty-first century, countermemory has surfaced in various popular cultural artifacts—ranging from visual depictions in TV shows and movies to music videos and art installations. For instance, music videos for Gary Clark Jr.'s "This Land" and Childish Gambino's "This Is America" employ different versions of countermemory to discuss race in the United States. Clark's video appropriates Confederate symbolism to say, as a Black man, "Fuck you, I am America's son." Gambino's video depicts hyperviolence against Black bodies to illustrate America's issues with gun violence, including the devaluation and vulnerability of BIPOC lives and the historical nature of that violence. Similarly, the critically acclaimed hit television show *Watchmen*, produced by Damon Lindelof, employs a racial countermemory lens—focusing on a white supremacist society and the history of racism in the United States. Lindelof's series thus counters traditional memories of not only the history of the nation but also comic books by deliberately racializing the story's world. The program *Lawman: Bass Reeves*, which highlights the life and accomplishments of Bass Reeves, the first Black US marshal, demonstrates how narratives that were considered "fringe" are now becoming a part of mainstream public memory (Cochran and O'Brien, 2024). Overall, in the new millennium, pop culture artifacts have reclaimed and countered white versions of American history and memory as well, illustrating how pervasive these narratives are even outside of memorial and academic spaces.

While the practice of disrupting dominant cultural narratives is not unique in American history, our purpose here is to bring to light areas where countermemory is becoming more commonplace, as well as to examine the tension between the rise in white supremacist rhetoric and countermemory as a response. Political shifts in the early 2000s represent a break between two distinct epochs in American life—one that celebrated the country's first Black president and one that demonstrated the deep-rooted white supremacy that clings to the country's collective psyche. This shift has engendered a resurgence of activism in response to white supremacist rhetoric, police brutality, and heightened xenophobic policies. We position countermemory within these activist movements as a rhetorical act of resistance. Countermemory can be material, digital, or a combination of the two. Whether countermemory is represented by a memorial to the victims of lynching where visitors can physically move their bodies among the names of those who were killed by racist violence or by a collection of blog posts that position the lived experiences of Black Americans at the center of study, this rhetorical movement is characterized by resistance and revitalizing narratives that are often whitewashed, lied about, or erased by hegemonic powers.

Why Us?

As coauthors, we came to work on countermemory from different perspectives, but we both understand its importance in today's society, especially in the way various local, regional, and national communities choose to remember or forget. We are inextricably tied to place. April now lives in East Texas, north of Houston, far from her roots in either Buffalo or South Carolina. James presently resides in rural Vermont, two thousand miles away from Grand Saline and his home state of Texas. Yet, even as we escape our homescapes, countermemory surrounds us.

When April moved to The Woodlands (about thirty miles north of Houston), she knew on some level that the issues she recognized in South Carolina would be present in her new home, but the extent to which this was so was far beyond her expectations. Soon after moving there, she came across a town called Tamina, one of the few African American settlements that still exist in the United States, a freedman's town that was established in 1871. Many residents are third- or fourth-generation Taminans. The community is known for taking care of itself despite its poverty and struggle for basic resources, including a sewer service (Tresaugue 2015). All these issues are particularly glaring in light of Tamina's material-geographic location, which is just a mile from the much wealthier The Woodlands. In addition, Tamina residents tell many stories about their freedman's status, there is no official public memory within the community—no historical markers, memorials, or monuments.

The more April sought out information about Tamina, the more she discovered that local historical commissions, like the Montgomery County Historical Commission (MCHC), intentionally omitted Black history from public memory. This led her to study the statewide historical agency, the THC, to determine how historical markers in the state of Texas discussed the lives and events of African Americans and other nonwhite individuals. In the case of Indigenous people, most of the historical markers tend toward negative remembrances. Prior to 2023, there were no historical makers that discuss lynchings, other racial terror, or the implications of Jim Crow laws. In 2016, the THC approved a marker titled "The Waco Horror Story," which chronicles the lynching of Jesse Washington. It was finally dedicated in a public ceremony in February 2023 (Saegert 2023). Many local activists argue that it is not accidental that the process took close to six years (Levada 2021). In Texas, any historical marker that addresses plantation homes purposefully avoids mentioning slavery (O'Brien 2021). In April's perspective, in light of the sheer volume of public memory artifacts in the state of Texas (far more than in any other state in the United States), the need for countermemory in Texas is urgent and necessary.

Similarly, James never imagined the countermemories that pervaded his hometown would follow him to Middlebury, Vermont, albeit in considerably less violent forms. At Middlebury College, the memories are not as brutal but are ever-present. When arriving from the town to Middlebury's campus, the first building a visitor sees is an old primary schoolhouse that the college bought in 1984. The school named the building after Alexander Twilight, the first Black American to earn a college degree in the United States and the first Black representative in a state house. He earned his degree from Middlebury in 1823, almost forty years before the US Civil War. When James joined the faculty at Middlebury in the fall of 2017, he soon learned of this history and was proud to be a part of a college with such a progressive past. However, he quickly learned that this history had been whitewashed for decades.

While it is true that Twilight is the first known Black American college graduate in the United States, this narrative erases several facts: Twilight could pass as white—the Middlebury administration of the 1820s did not know he had African ancestry—and the college first acknowledged Twilight's race in the 1980s as a means to claim the first Black graduate in the history of the United States and take the title away from a rival school, Amherst. While Middlebury's motivations are entirely polluted—and it is important to note these historical truths—a skeptic might interpret the story as one in which the college exploited the legacy for simple publicity. It makes sense that a Black (or perhaps biracial, since we do not know how he would identify himself) individual going to college in the early 1800s would need to pass as white. Of course a college would want to celebrate a historical first, but the publicity of Twilight at Middlebury feels superficial. While the college has issued an Alexander Twilight Historical Project that does a bit more truth-telling and reconciling for the campus, the realities of Twilight's ability to pass and the of the college's recognition of him in the 1980s are not on public display. Instead, they exist as counters to the simple celebration of Twilight at Middlebury.

We write this book both as a response to our pasts and educations and because countermemories followed us to our new homes and spaces. They are ever-present, even if we and others dare not to look. The countermemories of our pasts and presents molded us as rhetoricians, teachers, and scholars. They forced us to pay attention. We write them because of our obligations to our pasts, our memories, friends and families, and ourselves.

Conclusion

This book undertakes several movements in pursuit of examining dominant narratives in the United States—and more specifically, in the American South. We build a working theory of liberatory countermemory for rhetoricians by illustrating how its usage is already wide-sweeping and creates an exigence for future work. In what follows, we examine countermemory sites and artifacts in Texas and Georgia, introduce a spatialized application of countermemory called countermapping, explore how countermemory is enacted in pop culture, and present a countermemory tour of East Texas. Our intention is to make visible how countermemory sites and artifacts represent a rhetoric of resistance. In doing so, we critique both the heritage tourism industry in the American South and the mainstream public memory system that persistently exclude stories and resist truth-telling efforts. However, as Tim Gruenewald models in *Curating America's Painful Past*, we, too, do not want to disparage the progress that has been made over the early part of the twenty-first century in many heritage tourism sites. Many public memory workers, including historical interpreters, curators, tour guides, artists, and activists have made significant inroads at a time when any conversation about race and racism is labeled "CRT" or "woke" by the conservative Right. Our book is not intended to critique the progress that has been made but to present the gaps and persistent issues and to illustrate how and why countermemory functions in the United States.

In the epigraph for this introduction, we quote a proverb that Chinua Achebe attributes to Nigerian culture: "Until the lions have their own historians, the history of the hunt will always glorify the hunter." The same could be said of marginalized and racialized voices seeking to represent themselves and their histories via public memory artifacts. These collectives do not have the same power as the hunter (or normative white culture, in this case) to preserve their own memories. They get left behind, their memories only dictated via oral histories and small-scale, communal commemorations. However, the twenty-first century has so far borne witness to new memories and histories, ones that shine more light on stories that were forgotten and erased for decades, sometimes even centuries.

These stories come from the mouths of lions.

May this book reflect their perseverance.

1

Space, Place, and Materiality

A Model for Countermemory

Slavery museums exist around the world in places like Ghana, Nigeria, and England, and in December 2014, another one also opened in the United States. This museum, Whitney Plantation, may use the word "plantation" in its title, but the site functions in sharp contrast to most plantation tours in the US South. Where most plantation tours highlight the wealth and opulence of white owners of enslaved people, Whitney remembers the enslaved people who labored there via a variety of memorials built into the tour experience. Whitney turns an unshrinking gaze on the United States' relationship with slavery, similar to the approach that Germany has taken to remember the Holocaust. In fact, Mitch Landrieu, mayor of New Orleans from 2010–2018, called Whitney "America's Auschwitz," citing the similarities between the Holocaust and slavery, a comparison that many Americans are not willing to make (qtd. in Amsden 2015). Since the opening of Whitney, other slavery memorial sites have opened or are in the process of being built. Since the existence of slavery in US history is objectively true, why, then, is Whitney a model for countermemory? We only need to observe the plethora of anti-CRT bills being debated or already approved across many state legislatures in the US South at the time of this writing to understand the significance of a countermemory site like Whitney. Where Texas HB 3979 "prohibits teachers from presenting slavery as being a true principle of the founding of the United States but [that it] was a 'deviation' from the nation's ideals," Whitney presents slavery as an economic reality that shaped the country's foundation and engendered impacts that continue into our contemporary battles with systemic injustice (Casey 2021).

Like Whitney Plantation in purpose but not in scope, the African American Monument (AAM) in Savannah, Georgia, represents another model of countermemory. Since there are other monuments in the US South that memorialize Black history or people, the AAM may register as common or unexceptional.

However, when we examine the psycho-geographic landscape surrounding the monument, the long process that led up to its erection, and the way public memory is enacted in Savannah, it is clear that the AAM is a significant model for liberatory countermemory in terms of its impact. It is important to realize that the AAM was not initially accepted by the public memory workers in Savannah; in fact, the process of its erection took eleven years of contentious battles over its location and the wording on the facade. Not only that, but up until its unveiling in 2002, there was no public memory site that memorialized Black history in Savannah. This lack of representation is significant, especially given the fact that over 50 percent of the city's population identifies as Black and the city's role in the transatlantic slave trade as a port city. Also contributing to the AAM's significance as liberatory countermemory is Savannah's prominent role within southern public memory. Along with cities like Charleston and New Orleans, Savannah is recognized for its robust heritage tourism industry. Countless walking tours, carriage ride tours, ghost tours, house tours, twenty-two historic squares, Forsyth Park, and many other sites and artifacts inspire 14.8 million tourists to visit the city each year, which generates $3.1 billion in visitor spending ("Who We Are," n.d.). Clearly Savannah is a cultural epicenter of public memory, which makes the city's complex relationship with Black history even more compelling.

In this chapter, we turn to Whitney Plantation and the AAM as case studies of liberatory countermemory via site-based analysis. A comprehensive discussion of both sites cannot be accomplished in the scope of the chapter, so our examination focuses on specific areas. First, we focus on how the spatiality of these sites contributes to the overall rhetoricity, paying particular attention to the sites' psycho-geographic landscapes, which includes how the layout and organization advances the argument of the significance of the site. Second, we focus on the written text at each site, made up of markers, monuments, and informational text. Via discourse analysis, we identify how the sites present countermemory to the public. Finally, we highlight the materiality of both sites and draw attention to how their design and interactivity compel visitors to self-identify with the countermemory being communicated. Throughout the chapter, we argue that spatiality and materiality compel visitors to consider the differences between mainstream historical narratives and liberatory countermemory narratives, as well as contributing to the specific site's rhetoricity. Through these examples, we also demonstrate that while various racialized communities were mobilized to form these sites of liberatory countermemory, these spaces, places, and/or artifacts were often met with resistance and tension from white communities. While these case studies examine the specific nature of liberatory countermemory, we also use them to contrast local countermemories with dominant historical narratives, in a move that further depicts sites' rhetorical nature.

Organizing the Site-Based Analysis

To better understand the way countermemory functions in different sites and artifacts, we focus on three different aspects of memory at Whitney and three aspects of the AAM, all of which contribute to the overall rhetoricity of these sites. First, we examine eight statues and sculptures located around the grounds of Whitney. The variety of statues and sculptures (of both humans and nonhuman things) functions rhetorically to remind visitors in different ways and spaces of slavery's impact on "presentness of the past," an argument that public memory impacts present conditions (Legg 2005, 186). Moreover, the vitality of these statues and sculptures impacts the rhetorical ecologies present at Whitney and beyond; as Jenny Edbauer (2009) writes, "Life-as-network also means that the social field is not comprised of discrete sites but from events that are shifting and moving, grafted onto and connected with other events" (10).

We study the use of narrative and nonnarrative memorials via rhetorical and visual material analysis in two sites at Whitney, the anchor sculpture at the entrance and the series of statues that either depict aspects of the transatlantic slave trade or violence toward enslaved people who attempted a revolt in 1811 (for more about narrative and nonnarrative memory spaces, see Tim Gruenewald's *Curating America's Painful Past*). We note the similarities and differences in impact in these memorials based on their use of text and imagery, as well as their placement in the landscape and relationship with each other. Namely, we attend to the more expansive argument that Whitney makes via these memorials, an argument that centers the historicity of slavery as part of a larger conversation about racism and race relations in the United States—a goal that other sites of countermemory address as well, including the NMPJ and the Legacy Museum.

Second, we position the various memorials, sculptures, statues, landscape, and buildings as assemblages that communicate different messages when analyzed in conjunction with each other (Braidotti 2019, 6). Rather than just studying each element as a discrete form of rhetoric, we determine relationships between the artifacts, structures, and sites, a movement that highlights the ever-changing work of rhetoric as it interacts with humans and nonhumans. Furthermore, we find that the materiality of Whitney's memorials invites visitor introspection and relationality—or, as Propen (2012) says, these elements "act upon the minds and bodies" of visitors so that they experience each site with their whole bodymind (116). We draw out this concept at memorials like the Wall of Honor, which is composed of a reflective material that entreats visitors to see themselves (via their reflection) as they read the names and stories of enslaved people who labored at the plantation. We contrast Whitney's approach to engaging visitor identification with Dickinson, Ott, and Aoki's analysis of the Plains Indian Museum (PIM), which they find discourages such identification in favor of a rhetoric of reverence (2006, 28). Through the use of lights, sound, and language in each exhibit at the PIM, visitors are compelled to maintain a distanced, observational gaze and separate themselves from the stories and experiences of the Plains Indians. And instead of contemplating the impacts of colonization, Anglo visitors of the PIM admire the Plains Indians as people who lived long ago in a faraway land; as a result, they do not attend to contemporary issues of survivance and sovereignty (26–27). Through contrasting these sites, we demonstrate how Whitney Plantation creates opportunities for visitors to identify with enslaved people before, during, and after their tour—and to make connections to current issues of systemic racism that draw from these historical events. As a site of liberatory countermemory, Whitney overtly claims that "past pain [impacts] pain in the present" (Gruenewald 2021, 144).

Third, we juxtapose this tour in contrast with traditional heritage tours of historical homes, especially the way the big house is deemphasized and the humanity of enslaved people is highlighted at Whitney Plantation. Scholars in cultural geography, tourism studies, and rhetoric have shown repeatedly the problematic nature of many plantation tours. In many tours, enslaved people are not mentioned at all or only spoken of in outdoor spaces near enslaved quarters (Azaryahu and Foote 2008; Hanna et al. 2019). While it is becoming more common, like at McLeod Plantation or the Owens-Thomas House and Slave Quarters, many historic home tours only use the proper names of the white slave owners and do not perform the necessary research to uncover the names of enslaved people who labored at the site. However, at Whitney, the lives and experiences of enslaved people is the focus of the tour in terms of scope, time devoted, and emphasis. The owners of the enslaved, including their lifestyle and home, are relegated to a small portion of the tour. These choices communicate to visitors the importance of Black history, truth-telling, and as we argue, countermemory in a cultural landscape that repeatedly pushes back against these efforts.

In our analysis of the AAM in Savannah, which models liberatory countermemory on a smaller scale (in terms of its size but not its influence), we take a different approach. Due to its immense impact on establishing Black public memory in a white-dominated memoryscape, we first review the chronology of the monument. As part of our study, we consider the eleven-year battle to place the monument in Savannah and focus on the woman who spearheaded the efforts, Abigail Jordan. Since liberatory countermemory sites and artifacts are frequently contested, we find that it is valuable to assess the reasons why the monument was controversial and how Jordan and others addressed these concerns. Our analysis includes the cultural landscape of Savannah, focusing on the twenty-two town squares that memorialize white men, their locations, and how the AAM functions to disrupt these traditional memory sites by bringing attention to the transatlantic slave trade and the role the city of Savannah played in enslaving millions of Black Americans.

We make an important distinction, though: where a site like Whitney makes contemporary connections to systemic racism and does not attempt to "end on a positive note," the final version of the AAM focuses on positive elements, with imagery of the broken chains at the Black family's feet and the toned-down language carved into the stonework at the statue's base. This impulse to present a "rising up" narrative in Black public memory sites is well documented and can be seen at the National Museum of African American History and Culture. While the museum does depict slavery, lynching, Jim Crow laws, and other examples of racism and injustice, it does so on the floors below ground. When visitors enter the museum, they are confronted with mostly upbeat images and narratives of Black Americans like President Obama and Oprah, and the overall sweeping, bright architectural and design details are intended to present this narrative of "rising up," which also communicates that "liberation is complete" (Gruenewald 2021, 142, 146–47, 200).

A similar impulse is evident in Texas's Undertold Marker program, which is the THC's project to encourage residents to apply for historical markers that tell stories that have been underrepresented. At first glance, the program seems promising: since its inception in 2006, over one hundred markers have been placed that tell stories about Black, Latinx, and Asian American / Pacific Islander people and events ("Undertold Markers," n.d.). And while we do not want to minimize the significance of these markers, especially in a state with over sixteen thousand markers that highlight mostly white men, we also want to establish that these "undertold markers" tend to present a "rising up" narrative of marginalized groups instead of addressing the issues that caused the marginalization of these groups in the first place, like racism, discrimination, and the government-sanctioned violence that stemmed from these ideologies. We conclude our analysis of in this chapter by deliberating about the long-term impact of the AAM in Savannah and arguing that its placement in the city began a more robust countermemory movement in the city.

Whitney Plantation

Located thirty-five miles west of New Orleans, Whitney Plantation is situated on the west bank of the Mississippi River in St. John the Baptist Parish. While it is relatively close to New Orleans, Whitney feels worlds away from the hustle of the city's tourism industry. Aside from a handful of cottages, churches, and one or two gas stations, there is little activity between the city and Whitney. Moreover, on the approach to the plantation, the poverty of Louisiana's River Road, a road that stretches from New Orleans to Baton Rouge, is most apparent. River Road, also known as "plantation alley," is characterized by delipidated clapboard houses juxtaposed between opulent sugar plantations, a contrast that speaks to the state's poverty as well as to the unequal distribution of wealth that is directly linked to the slave trade (Elliott 2015).

While the American South now includes some civil rights memorials in addition to the Confederate memorials, as Erika Doss (2012) writes, "slavery is only tentatively represented in American memorial culture" (290). Although it may seem logical to house such a museum within the borders of a plantation house, as we have already indicated, these heritage tourism sites are instead largely used to circulate a narrative of the "Old South." Consequently, owner John Cummings's decision to turn the property into a slavery museum directly opposes the long history in the United States of remembering wealthy plantation owners, their furnishings, and a Lost Cause ideology while omitting/limiting discussions of slavery, enslaved individuals, or how their labor directly funded the country's early economy. We position Whitney Plantation as a site of countermemory that radically departs from plantation tours in the American South. In fact, Whitney's countermemory actively challenges heritage tourism dogma. While it is true that some plantation tours have begun to incorporate more Black history, including McLeod and Magnolia (both outside of Charleston), Whitney is distinct in that its entire purpose, in the words of Senegalese scholar Ibrahima Seck, is to make "reparations. Real reparations" (qtd. in Amsden 2015). Seck, who works alongside Cummings as the director of research for Whitney, explains that Cummings's goal in opening Whitney was to shift "the consciousness of others as his own has been altered" (qtd. in Amsden 2015). As with other sites of countermemory, like the NMPJ, Whitney's opening was met with protest from the white community, who argued that the tour would be too disturbing. In response, Cummings contends, "It is disturbing . . . But you know what else? It happened. It happened right here on this road" (qtd. in Amsden 2015).

Cummings's remarks illustrate one of Whitney's goals: to bring all visitors into the narrative and compel them to view history as a continuum—where past events continue to impact current conditions. Slavery is foundational to understanding our nation's history and it is important to recognize how it affects the lived experiences of people of color today. In an *Atlantic* article dedicated to Whitney Plantation, Cummings explains that "we live under the tremendous weight of slavery now. And this is not Black history that we are talking about; this is our national history" (qtd. in Rosenfeld 2015).

Statues, Sculptures, and "the Presentness of the Past"

The various statues and sculptures at Whitney communicate different narratives but all share a similar rhetorical function: to remind visitors of "the presentness of the past," that public memory directly informs our perspective of current events (and vice versa). While there are quite a few statues and sculptures at the site, here we highlight four, including the anchor located near the welcome center, the statues of enslaved children, the 1811 Slave Revolt Memorial, and a sculpture of the transatlantic slave trade.

Over the short walk from the parking lot to the visitor's center, visitors are immediately confronted with claims to knowledge via a dramatic metal sculpture of an anchor with chains to commemorate the slave trade (fig. 2). The anchor, which is surrounded by several feet of rusty chains, is a material reminder of the transatlantic slave trade. It also functions as a symbol of imprisonment, incarceration, and violence toward people of color in the United States. According to Christina Sharpe (2016), "the haunt of the [slave] ship envelops and persists in the contemporary" (60). By placing the anchor and chains at the entrance of the visitor's center, Whitney Plantation forces visitors to remember the chronological beginning of this story: individuals from Central and West Africa were loaded onto a ship as cargo, treated with inhumane violence, and suffocated in the ship's hold (55). But the symbolism of the chains (a motif that appears at other sites of countermemory like the AAM and the NMPJ) emphasizes to visitors that these issues have not been resolved and that Black Americans continue to live in the "wake" of slavery (5). Next to the sculpture is a pewter plaque that reads, "Every slave and every slave owner came to this place from different villages on different boats. Today we find ourselves all in the same boat awaiting another voyage. We must take the voyage together, regardless of the difficulty and the pain. Together we chart a course to a place where we can understand our part and find a cure for all evils brought here when the first boat visited our shore. Welcome to the Whitney" (fig. 3).

The text on the plaque means to be inclusive to all of those who were enslaved, either through the transatlantic or domestic trade. Whitney tells a story that is intended to be applicable in a variety of contexts. The tone then shifts to the present day: "Today we find ourselves all in the same boat awaiting another voyage," one that asks white Americans in antebellum America to recognize the role they played in our nation's history and to make this "journey" together with individuals who descended from slavery to "find a cure for all evils brought here." The evils obviously include racism and slavery, but the writers of this plaque undoubtedly include the injustices that persist in contemporary culture, including the mass incarceration of Black individuals, dramatic economic disparities between Black and white Americans, residential segregation, unequal educational opportunities, and other examples of structural racism that comprise the legacy of slavery. Taken together, the sculpture and the plaque position visitors as inside the problem of racism, unlike the "distanced, observational gaze" that Greg Dickinson et al. (2006) describe is a common feature of memory sites (28). Dickinson et al. explain that when sites of public memory deal with issues of violence and social issues, curators and creators of memory sites

Figure 2. Rusty anchor located near the entrance of Whitney Plantation; photograph by April O'Brien.

Figure 3. Plaque located outside entrance of Whitney Plantation; photograph by April O'Brien.

Figure 4. Statue of enslaved child at Whitney Plantation, located near the front door of recreated slave quarters. The slave cabins were acquired from nearby plantations and moved onto Whitney's land; photograph by April O'Brien.

often craft a distancing tone between visitors and the individuals or events that are being remembered. This allows white visitors to "avoid (or even forget)" the evils of racism, colonization, and slavery while still appearing to be respectful of people who have been harmed by this violence (29). Whitney, though, as a site of countermemory, diverges from these problematic patterns of remembrance and immediately compels visitors to consider their positionality.

In addition to the anchor sculpture, clay sculptures of enslaved children are positioned around the grounds. In the church, a few such sculptures are scattered around the sanctuary. These sculptures are, in the words of Jared Keller (2016), "a ghostly monument to [the children's] lost childhoods." The rhetorical impact of these statues is uncanny; they remind us both of the impact of slavery on children and of the effects of that institution that continue through each generation. Moreover, the vitality of these statues affects the rhetorical ecologies present at Whitney and beyond; as Edbauer (2009) writes, this vitality serves "to recontextualize those elements in a wider sphere of active, historical, and lived processes" (8). While Edbauer writes of events within a networked space, we also incorporate things and artifacts as elements that can be analyzed as in flux and in situ. A statue of an enslaved child within the larger assemblage of Whitney, including its memorials, its tour guides, and its overarching purpose to re/educate visitors about slavery, contains a multitude of meanings and implications, depending on who or what we "read" alongside the statue.

A similar statue, which exists near former slave quarters on the grounds of Whitney, is haunting in a different way. Studying a statue of an enslaved child alongside the Field of Angels memorial lets visitors learn about the brevity of life for many enslaved Black children (fig. 4). In this configuration, the child sits on the edge of the front porch, his gaze into the distance, his hands in his lap. In this composition, the child statue lingers both in the present and the past. What we mean by that is this: "The force of the present—and the core of its intelligibility—is that it does not coincide completely with the here and now" (Braidotti 2019, 6). Braidotti's words (as she draws from Felix Guattari) about vital materialism point to the continuum of material things—things like a statue of an enslaved child that stares out into the future—as they are subjects-in-process. Braidotti argues that we cannot differentiate the presentness of material things from the larger assemblage of space and time: "Approaching the present therefore produces a multi-faceted effect: on the one hand the sharp awareness of what we are ceasing to be [. . .] and on the other the perception [. . .] of what we are in the process of becoming" (6). When analyzed through the lens of Braidotti's observation, these statues become a continuous story about what it means to be Black in the United States, a story of injustice that did not end when slavery was abolished. This message is similarly echoed in the plaque near the anchor and chains at Whitney's entrance, as well as more explicitly through the messages

Figure 5. Memorial for German Coast uprising at Whitney Plantation; photograph by April O'Brien.

delivered by the tour guides. During April's guided tour, the historical interpreter frequently linked situations and experiences of the enslaved individuals with current examples of systemic racism. This rhetorical movement by Whitney is purposeful and speaks to the overarching goal of removing any distance(ing) from visitors. Visitors cannot distance themselves emotionally from the role of slavery in the nation's foundation; nor can they distance themselves in time from the impacts of slavery in current legislation or cultural acts.

This theme of visitor identification continues at other sites on the grounds, including the memorial for the 1811 German Coast uprising and a series of sculptures to commemorate the transatlantic slave trade (fig. 5). Like many events related to aspects of American chattel slavery, the 1811 German Coast uprising is not widely circulated in American public memory. The memorial on Whitney's grounds remembers the largest slave revolt in the US South, which took place from January 8–10, 1811, on the German Coast of Louisiana, a part of St. John's Parish (and Wallace, where Whitney is located). During that time, approximately five hundred enslaved people from St. Charles and St. John the Baptist Parishes banded together and collectively walked downstream toward New Orleans. On their journey of resistance, they killed two white men and vandalized the plantations they crossed. Local militia and other troops attacked the enslaved people, and many were killed in the battle. Others were executed via beheadings at the local plantations where they were owned. As a visual message to other enslaved people, "the heads were planted on poles at places where each of them had undergone punishment" ("The 1811 Slave Revolt Memorial," n.d.).

This memorial, created by Black artist Woodrow Nash, has been called "viscerally arresting" and "not for the kids" because of its graphic nature (Thrasher 2017; Amsden 2015). Nash's memorial recreates the beheadings through the presentation of sixty-three ceramic skulls on rods, with the name of each individual who was murdered on a plaque. Cumming intentionally placed the memorial near the big house (the last stop on the tour) because, in his words, "just in case you're worried about people getting distracted by the pretty house over there, the last thing you'll see before leaving here will be 60 beheaded slaves" (Amsden 2015). The disembodied nature of the memorial mirrors the physical act of beheading, of course, but it also reminds visitors of the commodification of Black bodies. Through both the material spaces and the narrative told by the tour guide, visitors are reminded that Black bodies were deemed worthless in society but had value as property. However, whereas this is discussed or remembered in most spaces throughout Whitney, nowhere else on the tour does one encounter such a tangible reminder of the brutality of slavery. Not only is the memorial an example of countermemory, as it remembers a revolt by the enslaved that is neither widely known nor taught in history books, but its proximity near the big house presents visitors with another embodied assemblage. Located on a plaque near the base of the memorial are these words: "Silence is requested." As part of Whitney's work to incorporate the whole body and mind into the experience, the assemblage reminds visitors to feel and experience the ideological weight of this memorial with silence.

The memorial is located at the entrance of a path that takes visitors past a series of sculptures visualizing aspects of the transatlantic slave trade. The order of these statues and sculptures is not chronological, which we believe is a rhetorical choice that compels the visitors' intellectual involvement. Some memorials at Whitney communicate overt narratives, usually via plaques or engraved text, and other sites compel visitors to ask questions—of themselves or of the sites themselves. This last section of the tour invites visitors to come to their own conclusions about the relationship between these memorials, sculptures, and statues. While there are likely many ways to interpret the order of the exhibits, one possible reading works counterchronologically. By beginning with the violence of the 1811 German Coast uprising, visitors first encounter one way that enslaved people resisted the institution of slavery. This last section of the tour, which presents examples of countermemory that dispel white-centric theories like American exceptionalism, is the effect—and the memorials that follow communicate the various causes of an event like the uprising.

Figure 6. "Hallelujah," created by Dr. Ken Smith; photograph by April O'Brien.

Figure 7. "Middle Passage," created by Dr. Ken Smith; photograph by April O'Brien.

Figure 8. "The Longboat," created by Ed Williams; photograph by April O'Brien.

While the uprising memorial in figure 5 portrays only the heads of the victims, the next statue shows a headless figure with exaggerated arms and hands that reach up in the air, possibly in prayer or supplication. The pose is liberatory, and the chains on each wrist are not connected, which again communicates freedom. When examined in situ, it is a response to the uprising memorial and is a plea for freedom in a space of bondage. The "Hallelujah" statue communicates the cry of enslaved people for equity and freedom (fig. 6). Just past this statue, Whitney continues to take visitors backward in time to "The Middle Passage" (fig. 7) This statue, an abstract retelling of the Middle Passage, exemplifies the violence and dehumanization of the forced voyage. Bodies are mingled together, and it is difficult to view where one person begins and another ends. In one place, hands reach out beyond the circle, which mirror the previous statue. Once visitors continue past the "The Middle Passage," they reach "The Longboat" (fig. 8). This sculpture also includes an informational plaque that provides necessary background, explaining that the longboat was a rowboat that was used by ship crews to collect enslaved people from Africa. The crew would round up captives and bring them on the longboat to the mouth of the river. Once there, the enslaved would be chained and kept in a "slave pen" until they were ready to be loaded onto the main ship. The informational plaque also notes that these humans were referred to as "cargo." In figure 8, the artist illustrates both the voyage and the bondage via the abstract boat and bar imagery. When we reassemble these four memorials, we see that Whitney begins with enslaved people in bondage and seeking to overthrow their oppressors. From there, visitors are reminded of enslaved people's continued battle for freedom over hundreds of years (if we interpret 1619 as the beginning of the slave trade in North America). Continuing backward in time, visitors view images of the Middle Passage and finally are confronted with how enslaved people were treated like cargo and rounded up on slave ships. In essence, Whitney reveals the story of racism and slavery in reverse order, inviting visitors to contemplate these injustices in a different way and consider the present-day implications of the enslaved trade—both on Whitney's land and all around the United States.

The Materiality of Whitney's Memorials

While we have highlighted the relationships between various memorials at Whitney and analyzed them as assemblages, it is also important to consider the role of materiality, especially in view of how materiality invites visitor identification—a theme repeated throughout the tour. The Wall of Honor, located at the beginning of the tour just after visitors view an introductory video at Antioch Baptist Church near the welcome center, features the names of 354 individuals enslaved at Whitney engraved on a row of stone walls. The inscriptions are in random order to demonstrate these persons' chaotic and tumultuous lived experience (Thrasher 2017). There were, of course, many more enslaved individuals than 354, but the museum only has a record of this number. In addition to the names, the memorial also includes information about individuals' country of origin as well as testimonials of the brutality they faced. One story recounts the violence and humiliation that enslaved children encountered: "When children used to get a whipping, they was taught to turn 'round and say, 'Thank you ma'am, for whipping me' and bow. That was mighty hard to do, but we were never allowed to pout. If we did we got another. And if we just needed being punished, we were put behind a door and had to stand on one foot until we were ready to say we were sorry" (fig. 9). Similar to other memorials with engraved names (like the Vietnam Veterans Memorial), the Wall of Honor is composed on a glossy, dark-colored granite surface. This kind of stone is naturally shiny and reflective, so it mirrors the sunlight, the surrounding greenery, and any individuals that stand nearby. It is on this reflective quality that we want to focus our analysis.

Figure 9. Wall of Honor, dedicated to all the people who were enslaved on Whitney Plantation; photograph by April O'Brien.

Figure 10. Reflection of April O'Brien in Wall of Honor; photograph by April O'Brien.

The materiality of this memorial draws the visitor into the experience, into the narrative being told. To read the names and the stories, the visitor must draw close to the wall. At that point, the visitor can read the text, but in between the spaces, the visitor sees herself—her reflection becomes part of the narrative (figure 10 shows April's reflection in the memorial). The assemblage of visitors, wall, text, and images once again compels the visitor to see herself as part of the narrative (similar to the text on the plaque near the anchor). Repeatedly, across Whitney's memoryscape, the rhetoricity of the nonhuman things—the statues, memorials, and plaques—invites the visitor to view herself as part of the story instead of drawing herself away from it. The mirrorlike quality of the Wall of Honor demonstrates the wall's vitality—what Bennett (2010) calls thing-power, which is "the curious ability of inanimate things to animate, to act, to produce effects dramatic and subtle" (6). Similarly, in Propen's analysis of the structures in the Lowell National Historical Park (2012), she focuses on the embodied nature of various sculptures and memorials, or the relationship between human visitors and nonhuman artifacts. For example, in her discussion of the park's Homage to Women sculpture, she notes that the sculpture "act[s] on visitors' bodies, inviting, or even requiring them to engage with it." Propen continues, "visitors bring their own contextualized, embodied experience to their readings of this sculpture" (115). Like the Homage to Women sculpture, the Wall of Honor becomes an embodied memorial experience. The visitor cannot separate herself from the narrative as she sees her reflection in the wall. The wall's thing-power becomes part of the rhetorical impact of this memorial, and like the other spaces and places that we analyze in Whitney, draws the visitor into the experience instead of distancing her from its darkness. Countermemory enmeshes visitors into narratives that have otherwise been erased from America's public memory, where traditional memory sites dissociate visitors from what is being remembered.

Disrupting Historical Home Tours

To capture the spatiality and texture of Whitney Plantation, we use a critical spatial perspective and highlight features of the tour, with extended analyses of specific memorials. These memorials distinguish Whitney from most heritage tours designed by agents of memory in the South just as much as the content of the tour itself does. A typical plantation tour begins in the big house, and visitors spend the majority of the time in and around the mansion (Hanna et al. 2019; Azaryahu and Foote 2008). These tours are, above all, a tour of a house and the immediate grounds. Whitney disrupts the plantation tour genre across multiple registers. Not only does it flip the narrative and focus on the individuals who were enslaved, but it combines the genre of memorial and tour. Specifically, the tour is spread out over a few acres and includes eight memorials intended to capture the names and histories of the individuals who labored there, as well as around the state of Louisiana. We view these memorials as part of Whitney's assemblage, which is part of the larger psychogeographic memory of Louisiana's participation in slavery. Many of these memorials feature statues, plaques, and other signage that entangles visitors into complex relationships between themselves and these artifacts/things (Todd 2016, 6).

In their examination of two antebellum plantation tours, Stephen Hanna et al. (2019) studied the relationship between the ordering of space and narrative. Using narrative mapping, Hanna and his colleagues were able to plot how traditional plantation tours "give voice and legitimacy to certain historical actors and interpretations while eliding others" (49). In one of their case studies at Berkeley Plantation, they found that docents and visitors used vague and distancing language to discussed enslaved individuals or the concept of slavery, in sharp contrast to the language used about the owners of the enslaved: "Observers noted that when guides and visitors mentioned Berkeley's enslaved population, they only discussed basic facts, such as the number of slaves the Harrisons owned or the labor performed by enslaved persons. Some observers found that guides used passive voice, such as 'there were 110 slaves,' or deployed words like 'servants' and 'they.' Guides never named enslaved individuals, did not provide humanizing details about their lives, and did not attempt to engage visitors emotionally on the topic. This contrasts with the rich biographical details visitors learn about members of the Harrison family" (9). These findings fit with expectations and also match April O'Brien's study of Woodburn Plantation in Pendleton, South Carolina. Her tour of Woodburn was a private tour, and the docent had foreknowledge about her research about Pendleton's Black history. Even with this knowledge, the docent spent most of the tour delineating the slave owner family's opulent lifestyle. When she discussed the enslaved individuals, she explained that one reason that the kitchen was located in an outbuilding was because the enslaved could not be trusted to not burn the house down, since they were not used to such fine furnishings. She also attempted to downplay the humiliation and lack of freedom that the enslaved experienced, citing their freedom to move around the region at night while the owner and his family slept (O'Brien 2019). These examples, along with Hanna et al.'s, illustrate the typical features of plantation tours in southern heritage sites, which include the docents' focusing on the wealth and material possessions of the owners the enslaved, centering the big house and immediate grounds, dehumanizing the individuals who labored at the plantation, and using euphemisms for "slave" like "worker" or "laborer." While an increasing number of plantation tours now include the perspective of enslaved individuals and even provide names and narratives, Whitney diverges from these by remaking the plantation tour into a slavery museum.

After visitors spend over an hour walking around the grounds on a guided tour, they spend fifteen minutes at the big house. Rather than beginning at this site, Whitney tour ends there, and this last stop somehow seems inconsequential when compared to the stories presented throughout the tour. This decision is a rhetorical one: it explicitly demonstrates the impact of countermemory when employed in typical southern heritage sites. Keeping the big house at the end of the tour functions to footnote what is usually the highlight of a plantation tour. In doing so, Whitney enacts the principles of countermemory. It replaces a dominant hegemonic narrative with the perspective of those who were enslaved. It poignantly remembers the injustices that the American South has attempted to conceal. And it materially links the past with the present, through the clay sculptures of enslaved children, the various memorials on site, and the open discussion with Whitney's docents. Whitney Plantation represents an important feature of liberatory countermemory—a rhetoric of countermemory that subverts and rewrites heritage tourism sites in a way that could be transformative in the American South.

African American Monument

Much of the American South has chosen to valorize Confederate soldiers and the Lost Cause, and the result has been the explicit erasure of Black history. Some argue that this willful rejection is due to shame about the institution of slavery. Even if that was true, countries like Germany have channeled similar shame into creating various memorials and monuments that compel visitors to experience the loss and grief of the Holocaust. Until relatively recently, the United States has hesitated to follow suit, except for in selected locations. Still, in the twenty-first century, various examples of countermemory have cropped up the American South, as seen in Kristan Poirot and Shevaun Watson's analysis of urban slavery sites Charleston, South Carolina, or James Chase Sanchez and Kristen Moore's study of a defaced Confederate memorial, also in Charleston. In what follows, we highlight Savannah's African American Monument.

In 2002, Savannah erected its first Black memory site that openly acknowledges slavery; it is also one of the nation's few public sculptures that depicts slavery (Doss 2012, 287). The city of Savannah is rich in historical narratives and sports forty-three monuments—none of which, prior to the AAM, dealt with slavery or Savannah's role in the trade of enslaved people (Alderman 2010, 95). Concerned about the city's tourism industry, officials did not want this monument to be the first thing tourists saw when they disembarked from their tour boat. Some Black residents and officials, too, were concerned that the monument would stir up racial conflict because of the language used on the memorial (91). Indeed, together with some other scholars, Doss argues that there is a relationship between a national sense of shame and the politics of remembering/

forgetting slavery: "Today, shame about the nation's transgressions is generally absent in terms of how most Americans think about themselves and the nation [. . .] To acknowledge shame, after all, is to admit that there is something to be ashamed about. And for many Americans, shameful monuments in the nation's past are just that—in the past and therefore removed from present personal and/or collective understandings of relevance and responsibility" (Doss 2012, 256). Savannah's vibrant tourism industry has played a significant role in the city's outward conversation about its history. To acknowledge slavery, the city would have to acknowledge the shame that accompanies this period. Emotions like sadness, anger, and shame do not go well with the tourism industry, so rather than facing these historical events with transparency, Savannah avoided and erased—until the AAM was crafted. As cultural geographer Kenneth Foote (2003) observes, "shame can be a powerful motive to obliterate all reminders of tragedy and violence," and as a result, memories that remind white Americans of brutality and injustice become invisible in the national landscape (174).

A retired educator named Abigail Jordan fought for eleven years to get this monument erected. Jordan describes the challenges she overcame: "I have been bloodied in my struggle to get that memorial put up. Not literally bloodied, but figuratively. They've [the city of Savannah] even got a statue of a dog" (Buncombe 2002). Here, Jordan refers to the fact that, in addition to the twenty-two historic squares, historical markers, and walking tours that remember white men, Savannah placed a statue of a girl, Florence Martus, and a dog on River Street (Berinato 2021). Jordan's meaning is clear: at the time, the city was willing to erect any kind of monument or memorial, as long as it did not deal with Black history. After intense debates over the monument's appearance, the text that would appear on it, and its location, the AAM was revealed to the public in 2002. Designed by Savannah artist Dorothy Spradley, a white professor from Savannah College of Art and Design, the monument stands nearly eleven feet tall, with a granite base. It depicts a family of four African Americans in contemporary clothing; they stand close together, a circle of broken chains at their feet (fig. 11). The figures are positioned to face Africa and the Savannah River; the latter's location in proximity to the Atlantic Ocean promoted the city's significant role in and benefit from the economic profits that came from the slave trade (Alderman 2010, 96; "African-American Monument" n.d.; Doss 2012, 287). On the bottom of the monument is this inscription, taken from speeches of Maya Angelou that were recited and adapted about the Middle Passage: "We were stolen, sold and bought together from the African continent. We got on the slave ships together. We lay back to belly in the holds of the slave ships in each other's excrement and urine together, sometimes died together, and our lifeless bodies thrown overboard together. Today, we are standing up together, with faith and even some joy."

Figure 11. "African American Monument" by artist Dorothy Spradley. Erected in 2002 in Savannah, Georgia; photograph by April O'Brien.

Both the discursive and nondiscursive elements of the monument contribute to its rhetorical impact. Not all monuments include text, and when they do, the text is often limited in length. In this case, though, the text is significant, when we consider it in terms of the polemic it caused in Savannah and in terms of the revisions it underwent. James Loewen (1999) writes, "To understand a marker or monument we must not only analyze what it says and how it looks but also when it was unveiled" (22). The initial version (which does not include the last line from the final version cited above) referred to images from the Middle Passage, and many stakeholders were concerned that it was too graphic, that it would harm tourism and stir up racial conflict ("African-American Monument" n.d.; Alderman 2010, 91; Buncombe 2002). One visitor from South Carolina wrote a letter to the editor of the *Savannah Morning News* expressing his dismay over the proposed text: "The monument, with its inscription describing lying in excrement and urine, is bound to wipe the smile off the face of the giddiest tourist, and I suspect that many will follow my example and avoid

River Street in the future" (qtd. in Alderman 2020, 96–97). Many Black community leaders were also concerned about the inscription on the monument—they supported a memory site for the city's Black history, but they feared that the explicit nature of Angelou's writing would polarize and divide the community (Buncombe 2002). Eventually, the parties involved were able to come to a compromise, though, in the form of an additional sentence that would provide a message of hope: "Today, we are standing up together, with faith and even some joy." This last statement reflects the "rising up narrative" that Gruenewald (2021) unpacks in the National Museum for African American History and Culture. The revised statement illustrates the city's goal to "frame memory of painful and traumatic past in a way that offers an uplifting resolution" (113).

The conflict surrounding the original text demonstrates the far-reaching effects of dominant cultural narratives in the American South. At the beginning of the introduction, we discussed John Gast's painting *American Progress* and how it illustrates an abiding narrative about the United States. This narrative paints white men as the heroes of our national story and people of color as those who threaten the advancement of the nation. Angelou's words, while an accurate portrayal of the slave trade, are viewed as endangering not just Savannah's public identity but the larger story that the American South believes about itself. Thus, the inscription caused friction in the community, so much so that even many Black residents were not in favor of the monument. Recall that prior to 2002 there was no public signage of any kind in Savannah that depicted the city's role in the slave trade—not a single marker, memorial, monument, or tour. The city's refusal to remember its Black history or accurately portray its involvement in the slave trade—the active absence of this memoryscape—is remarkable and noteworthy, especially when we study how Black residents initially felt about the monument. Their hesitancy did not stem from discomfort with the language used; it originated from a fear of overt racism and violence from white community members who opposed the monument. Fear of white retribution is based on historical experience and is widely recognized through historical documentation and the lived experiences of African Americans (Loewen 2005).

In addition to the inscription, the nondiscursive elements of the monument contribute to its rhetorical affect and influence. Many monuments in the United States communicate the value of white individuals and the inferiority of people of color strictly via the configuration of the monument. Monuments like "The Good Darky" in Baton Rouge, Louisiana, were intended to further the cause of white supremacy by depicting Black Americans' "faithful devotion and historical subordination" (Loewen 1999, 204). The monument that until January 2022 stood in front of the American Museum of Natural History in Manhattan portrayed Theodore Roosevelt on a horse with an African man on one side of him and a Native American man on the other. Roosevelt's left hand rested on the African man's head, and the Native American simply walks alongside the horse. The statue was removed because of its overt colonial symbolism. In New Orleans, a monument for the "founder" of the city, Jean Baptiste LeMoyne de Bienville, presents Bienville standing proudly, gazing off into the distance introspectively. There are two men at his feet: one Native American sitting with his gaze downward, and a monk reading a Bible. In both the Roosevelt and LeMoyne sculptures, the white individual is larger than and spatially above the people of color represented. Loewen (1999) argues that these monuments are a "declaration of white supremacy," both in terms of how they are visually presented as well as the circumstances surrounding their creation (31).

We contrast the AAM with these examples to highlight the significance of a memory site that does not present people of color as inferior to white Americans. Likewise, while the inscription discusses slavery and the slave trade, the monument does not portray enslaved people. Instead, the individuals are a contemporary Black family: a father, mother, and two children. The family stands close together, curving into each other and holding on to each other. The father and son gaze outward, toward the water, and the mother and daughter look inward, toward each other. The tone and mood of this monument are markedly different from those of many of the monuments that feature people of color. Instead of kneeling beside white men or bowing their heads, the family featured in this monument stands tall, banding together in strength. The chains, reminiscent of the art installation near Whitney Plantation's entrance, no longer hold this family in bondage—rather, they collect around their feet. Because of the eleven-foot height of the monument, the inscription along its granite base, and the open space surrounding it, visitors are compelled to look up at the family, walk around the monument, and bend down to read the inscription. To consider possible readings for the AAM, visitors must walk its circumference, and in so doing, view the family from all angles. As they walk around the memorial, the visitors can notice the direction the family is facing: toward the waterways, toward the slave ships, toward Africa. This movement acts on visitors' bodies, and as a result, visitors are encouraged to bring their own meaning to the monument. All these elements heighten the monument's rhetorical impact and promote a sense of contemplation, pride, strength, and hope. Even without the inscription, the materiality of this monument enacts countermemory in a city that—up until 2002—did not publicly acknowledge its African American heritage. Bennett (2010) contends that an object's thing-power "draws attention to an efficacy of objects in excess of human meanings, designs, or purposes they express or serve" (20). As part of a larger psychogeographic network, the monument demonstrates the impact of countermemory within communities.

Between 2002—when the AAM was built—and 2019—when Abigail Jordan was honored for her advocacy work—many changes occurred on Savannah's public memory scene that demonstrate the rhetorical influence of countermemory on the community. Of the twenty historical markers in Savannah that note African American individuals or historical events related to them, five were erected prior to or in 2002. The other fifteen were built after the AAM ("Explore," n.d.). None of the markers built prior to 2002 discuss slavery, Jim Crow, segregation, or the civil rights movement. However, after the AAM was built, many of the new markers openly discussed slavery, including the largest sale of enslaved people in Georgia's history, where 436 individuals were sold. This marker, built in 2008, refers to this time as "the weeping time" in African American history and also overtly mentions the fact that families were separated ("Largest," n.d.). In 2016, another marker, part of the larger Georgia Civil Rights Trail, highlights the Savannah Protest Movement and the labor of many individuals to fight for equality in Savannah ("Georgia Civil Rights Trail," n.d.). In addition to these changes in Savannah's memoryscape, in 2017, the city developed a task force, titled the Confederate Memorial Task Force, to make a decision about the Confederate memorial in Forsyth Park. This task force began its work a couple of months after the Charlottesville riots in Virginia. The committee of seven individuals, ranging from academics to community leaders to tour guides, comprised only two Black participants. After completing research about the matter, the task force put forward eight recommendations, which included swapping out the term "Confederate" with "Civil War." None of the recommendations envisioned significant changes to the landscape of Forsyth Park, a memoryscape that pays homage to the Confederacy within its perimeters (O'Brien 2023). At the same time, at the conclusion of the report, the authors write, "Savannah needs to expand its Civil War interpretation throughout the city, as well as the contributions to Savannah by African Americans, such as Susie King Taylor, March Haynes, and Rachel Brownfield. The dialogue regarding additional memorials and monuments needs to be ongoing; there are other stories to be told throughout town" ("Confederate Memorial" 2017). These changes (and changes in the following decades) to Savannah's public memory demonstrate the ripple effects from the AAM in 2002.

Conclusion

Whitney Plantation and the AAM demonstrate the spatiality and texture of countermemory, especially when examined through the lens of materiality and a critical spatial perspective. Enacting countermemory through our citational practices and theoretical framework, we draw from a wide range of interdisciplinary scholarship, including the work of Todd, TallBear, Kimmerer, and from the new materialism, including Bennett, Gries (2015), and Rickert, as well as

Propen's visual-material rhetorics. While citational practices have been examined by scholars (Clary-Lemon 2019; Druschke 2019; Sackey et al. 2019; Towns 2018), there is still much work to be done to promote equality and to redress these injustices. Along the same lines, we draw from cultural geography in our study of the rhetoricity of spaces and places and apply a critical spatial perspective to better understand the relationship between sites of countermemory and the surrounding psychogeographical landscapes. A critical spatial perspective is key to our site-based analysis because it studies how issues of race, racism, and settler colonialism impact spaces and places. In terms of our site analysis, using both materiality and a critical spatial perspective provides a more holistic understanding of each space or place.

While Whitney Plantation and AAM differ in terms of scope and impact, each is instructive as a model of countermemory. As with many countermemory sites or artifacts, both sites were met with resistance from local community members and even national sources. Both portray slavery, but as we have discussed, do so with varying methods. Where Whitney compels visitor identification and offers an honest presentation of the violence, horror, and injustice of the transatlantic slave trade, the AAM falls back on a "rising up" narrative in some capacity. Yet, both sites generate an openness to countermemory, especially in conjunction with the Black Lives Matter movement. In addition to increasing numbers of countermemory sites in Savannah, over the last two decades there has been a growth in Black history walking tours and a greater focus on Gullah Geechee remembrance. One of the most popular historic homes, the Owens Thomas House, which historically exploited Black slave labor, revamped its tour to focus equally on the lives and experiences of enslaved people—and changed the name to the Owens-Thomas House and Slave Quarters (Browning-Mullis 2022). Likewise, the opening of Whitney has led other plantation tours to portray enslaved people's narratives more honestly in Louisiana and in the American South overall (Amsden 2015).

These sites also further highlight the importance of presences and absences as a quality of liberatory countermemory. The historical absence of any mention of enslaved people or slavery in many spaces in the American South emphasizes the resistance to claim and understand our national sins even on a local scale. It is easier for most to move past these memories, to argue they have no value to today, than to sit with them and let our memories rub against reality. Yet, poignantly, Whitney and the AAM also establish how increasing the presence of liberatory countermemories begets more countermemories. When we move to acknowledge the power of these memories in such spaces and actually construct memorials to honor the enslaved and the memory of slavery, we create room for more countermemories to flourish. Their very emergence constructs a space for more acknowledgement.

In our next chapter, we turn to countermapping, an application of a critical spatial perspective, to demonstrate how countermemory can be used to rethink overlapping concepts of mapping and memory. The practice of countermapping can be extended into other nontraditional modes of expression; we use this chapter to illustrate how new mapping practices resist hegemonic memories often found in maps.

2

Countermapping

A Spatially Diagrammed Resistance

According to cultural geographer Denis Cosgrove (1999), maps are complex and ambiguous artifacts (2). Cosgrove, along with many other cultural geographers and critical cartographers, asserts that maps are also inaccurate, distorted, and socially oppressive. Cartographer John Nelson (n.d.) created a story map that highlights common mistakes people make when imagining maps. For example, in most of our traditional maps, continents are misplaced: even though many maps position it in the southern hemisphere, directly across from South America, most of Africa is actually located north of the equator. While misplacements are problematic, Nelson notes an even more disturbing issue—the Mercator projection, which is the most common type of map found in classrooms in the United States, distorts the shape and size of continents and countries. Brazil appears to be quite diminutive, but the country is larger than Canada. Greenland looks to be about the same size as Africa, but in reality, Africa is fourteen times larger than that island (Nelson n.d.; Mason 2018). These examples, which are not exhaustive, demonstrate the imprecision of many maps on a global scale. Rhetorically, when people perceive continents like Africa as significantly smaller than they are, they might likewise consider them as less important or worthwhile (since, for some reason, for many folks size equals power). All this is to say that it is completely logical, and almost expected, that maps tell a one-sided story that the general public believes as objective truth.

Maps are one of the oldest, and certainly most widely accepted, forms of public memory. They are the preface to a much larger story of life, and the way we set up the story defines how it will be told. Since maps are so influential in shaping public perception of place, memory, and identity, it is crucial to countermap public memory—so we can visualize the memories that have been omitted and forgotten. Historically, though, maps have hindered decolonization and anti-racist efforts by communicating false spatial knowledge and undermining the contributions of people of color in human geographies. While maps are rendered as artifacts that present objective information, cultural geographers characterize them as being complex, ambiguous, inaccurate, and socially oppressive (Cosgrove 1999, 2). To support this perspective of maps, Jim Enote, a traditional Zuni farmer and tribal member, makes this compelling argument: "More lands have been lost to Native peoples through mapping than through physical contact" (qtd. in Loften and Vaughan-Lee 2019). Enote's statement underscores the impact of maps and mapping on the survivance and sovereignty of Indigenous people both in the United States and throughout the Global South. While maps have contributed to the colonization and displacement of Indigenous people, maps and map-making practices have also marginalized Black communities and their geopolitical concerns through geographies of exclusion (McKittrick and Woods 2007, 4).

As a result, scholars, activists, and artists have taken up disruptive mapping practices to resist dominant spatial narratives—a practice called countermapping. The term "counter-mapping" has been used by scholars Derek Alderman, Joshua Inwood, and Ethan Bottone, as well as by Indigenous activists like Jim Enote. We use the term as a countermemory method/ology and act of resistance. Sarah Radcliffe (2011), a cultural geographer who specializes in decolonial geographies in Ecuador, describes how Shuar, Achuar, and other Indigenous people employ "map-making as a critical tool in their struggles for postcolonial justice" (129). Likewise, artists like Terrance Guardipee, Chris Pappan, and Jaune Quick-to-See Smith create "spatial disruptions" and recenter Native geographies in their work (Barnd 2017, 110). Jeff Littlejohn, a historian and scholar who focuses on public history, composed an interactive map/website called Lynching in Texas, which incorporates a map of hundreds of lynchings in Texas along with archival information about these events. These artifacts, which include interactive maps, paintings, and websites, illustrate the various ways in which countermapping can be employed.

This chapter picks up on a concept introduced in chapter 1, a critical spatial perspective, which orients maps as "quintessentially ideological" artifacts that demonstrate the role of power and agency (Barton and Barton 2004, 234; Hawthorne 2019, 5; McKittrick 2011, 5–6). Instead of viewing maps as neutral or apolitical, "critical spatial perspectives reveal inequitable power relationships in the ways space is used, remembered, and communicated" (O'Brien 2020b). In what follows, we describe a specific kind of critical spatial perspective that, following other scholars and activists, we call countermapping. As a spatial application of countermemory, countermapping seeks to disrupt racist and colonial forms of spatial representation by 1) opposing white, American exceptionalist views of spatial history or memory and 2) visually representing public inequalities, tragedies, or injustices that have been forgotten or erased.

To set the methodological foundation for countermapping, we turn to Indigenous geographies and Black feminist geographies, two subfields of cultural geography concerned with issues of settler colonialism, representation, power, and space-making. We also tell the story of the "spatial turn" in humanities research (including rhetoric studies) and position countermapping as a spatially diagrammed resistance. The chapter is informed by the following research questions: 1) What is the purpose of and significance of countermapping to both Indigenous and Black communities? 2) How is a critical spatial perspective representative of countermemory? 3) What are the similarities and differences between decolonial artistic, anti-lynching persuasive, and interactive embodied countermaps? Overall, countermaps disrupt the physical boundaries of colonization and reinscribe tribal memory, allowing people to rethink how spatial stories are told to make visible collective memories that have been erased by dominant white culture.

The "Spatial Turn" and Critical Spatial Perspectives

Cosgrove (1999) acknowledges that mapping is a "deceptively simple activity" because maps have been historically viewed as transparent or as a neutral informative transfer (1, 3). However, scholars in cultural geography maintain that maps are also ideological and depict what a culture wants to remember (Barton and Barton 2004; Cosgrove 1999; Harley 2002; McKittrick 2011). As Amy Propen (2012) articulates, maps are "always in flux" as they "respond to . . . shifting contexts and relations" (11). This interpretation of maps, reflecting a critical spatial perspective, views maps as "opaque" artifacts that involve choices, submissions, uncertainties, and intentions and likewise change our perception of spaces and places (Cosgrove 1999, 3, 7). Many cultural geographers turn to Michel Foucault's (1977) research on power to establish a critical spatial perspective, but as rhetoricians also interested in critical cartography, our task is more expansive: we investigate the role of positionality, privilege, and power (Jones et al. 2016; Walton, Moore, and Jones 2019). While often used interchangeably, each of these concepts is distinct: whereas positionality determines "what our identity means in particularly contexts of action," privilege influences "the types and extents of unearned advantages we are accorded, and power governs an individual or group's agency in relation to their positionality and privilege" (Walton, Moore, and Jones 2019, 63; Jones, Moore, and Walton 2016, 220). And power shifts depending on a person's positionality and privilege. The roles played by decolonization and settler colonialism, representation and power, and Black place-making are key to assessing how positionality, privilege, and power is enacted in spatial spheres.

Since maps are rhetorical, they "allow [us] to see relationships between spaces and objects that [we] would not be able to see otherwise" (O'Brien 2020a;

Propen 2012, 6). Thus, we recognize that maps are impacted by a variety of social, cultural, ideological, and rhetorical contexts—and, alternatively, maps also shape these same contexts (O'Brien 2020b; Propen 2012, 6). Maps create meaning. They construct meaning through using specific cartographic conventions, including the use of grids, icons, and symbols; it is also important to note how scale is used to highlight some places and minimize others (Propen 2012, 11). As Nedra Reynolds (2004) writes, maps are deemed valuable by how they represent "reality," or what a culture establishes as significant (81). In this sense, Tamara Butler (2018) argues that "since Black women experience oppressions along the lines of space, place, race, gender, sexuality, and class, liberation should be imagined along those same lines" (28). Black girl cartography, a praxis-oriented framework that Butler employs, studies "how and where Black girls are physically and sociopolitically mapped in education" (29). Ultimately, Butler's work "charts resistance," by emphasizing how geography magnifies the social inequities that Black women experience (30). Just as Butler's Black girl cartography activates resistance, Samantha Senda-Cook, Michael Middleton, and Danielle Endres (2018) argue for a method of rhetorical cartographies to counteract the tendency for marginalized communities to be elided by mapping practices. In their chapter about Omaha's demographic segregation, these three scholars contend that because place is a concept in flux, embodied mappings of spaces and places can "select, reflect, and deflect" through community experiences. Likewise, Elise Verzosa Hurley (2018) draws an important connecting line between cultural geography and technical communication and argues that these fields can "mutually inform and enrich each other" (108).

Additionally, many cultural rhetoricians, who focus on the "multiple, mutually-informing, and overlapping ways in which rhetoric and culture interface," have studied spatial practices from a decolonial perspective or from the perspective of Black place-making (Cobos et al. 2018, 141). In Malea Powell's 2012 Conference on College Composition and Communication Chair's address, she centers the relationship between stories and place: "Stories take place. Stories practice place into space. Stories produce habitable space" (391). Powell (2012) describes a direct connection between stories and space, a rhetorical movement that many other cultural rhetoricians articulate in their research as well. For example, Chicana rhetorician Gabriela Raquel Ríos (2019) examines the relations between land, language, and people through the lens of Andean relational ontologies, a research object that aligns well with the goals of Indigenous geographers (384). Ríos considers *khipus*, which are "knotted cord systems functioning as interfaces that hold census data as well as history," and discusses how one role of *khipus* is to salvage material from the land destroyed by colonial violence (384–85). In that way, *khipus* represents a map of Tupicochan memory and identity in material form. In their extensive community-engaged multimodal project with the Iowa tribe in Oklahoma, Rachel Jackson and Phil Bratta (2020) layer images of the "land run" in 1893 to demonstrate University of Oklahoma's complicity in settler colonialism. By chronicling their research process, including working with the Institutional Research Board, Jackson and Bratta map the memory of the Iowa tribe as part of the larger memoryscape of Oklahoma. Likewise, while not explicitly about maps or mapping, Lisa King's ongoing project to reclaim American Indian mound sites and Andrea Riley-Mukavetz's land-based "snake stories" (2020) both illustrate a cultural rhetorics approach that considers relations between people, things, and land. For their part, Eve Tuck and K. Wayne Yang (2012) argue that settler colonialism has "mark[ed] the organization, governance, curricula, and assessment of . . . learning" (2). Parallel to that claim, they contend that settler colonialism also impacts "what counts as knowledge" as a way to maintain inequitable social structures (2). It is from this framework that Indigenous geographies pursue goals of self-determination and cultural continuity and reject settler colonialism and Native dispossession (Barnd 2017, 2).

Also in this vein, Katherine McKittrick (2011) has argued that "Black matters are spatial matters" (xiii), a statement that reflects "the complex spatialities of Black life, oppression, resistance, and radical imagination" (Hawthorne 2019, 2). While the field of geography has much work to do to recognize Black geographies (not unlike the need for more recognition of the role of BIPOC scholarship in rhetoric studies), the 2018 American Association of Geographers (AAG) Annual Meeting choose Black geographies as its theme, with the theme committee providing the following statement about race and place: "Practices of Black life, resistance, and survival are inseparable from the production of space. Decades of work within and beyond the discipline have centered Black Geographies frameworks in re/considering humanness, cities, regional blocs, social movements, faith, identities, and structural inequalities. Black-oriented epistemologies operate in resistance to reductionary claims on Black spaces, places, theories, and methods" (AAG Call for Papers). As an interdisciplinary praxis, countermapping draws from these conversations to establish a framework. Indeed, as McKittrick (2011) contends for a "Black sense of place," countermapping, too, promotes a spatialized reckoning that visualizes an inclusive and diverse sense of place (949).

Countermapping, though, is best understood as an interdisciplinary method/ology that draws from various frameworks and theories. When it is employed as a method, countermapping takes many forms, so it is best to keep it as a fluid, loosely defined method. While it is diverse in its application, countermemory maintains two distinct purposes: first, it opposes white, American exceptionalist views of spatial history or memory, and second, it visually represents public inequalities, tragedies, or injustices that have been forgotten or erased.

Representation and Power

Eve Tuck and K. Wayne Yang (2012) argue that settler colonialism has "mark[ed] the organization, governance, curricula, and assessment of . . . learning" (2). Parallel to that claim, they contend that settler colonialism also impacts "what counts as knowledge" as a way to maintain inequitable social structures (2). It is from this framework that Indigenous geographies pursue goals of self-determination and cultural continuity and reject settler colonialism and Native dispossession (Barnd 2017, 2). Settler colonialism is defined as "a form of colonialism wherein nonindigenous or 'settler' populations implant themselves in new lands" (9). If we think back to our description of John Gast's painting in the introduction, we can see how the work exemplifies settler colonialism (fig. 1). The settlers take up three-fourths of the painting and all demonstrate their "stake" in the land. Some settlers are farming, and others are traveling via Conestoga wagon, the latter emphasizing the fact that Native Americans were increasingly driven from their lands. Furthermore, as Natchu Barnd (2017) writes, "Settlers initiate a fundamental transformation in the demographics, cultures, and physical landscape of colonized lands" (9). This, too, is apparent in Gast's painting whether by settler farming, the introduction of pollution via railroads, or the "smoothing" of the land that the painting depicts. Indeed, in the painting, the land on which settlers reside appears to be brighter and flatter, friendlier and more familiar, than the land in the rest of the image. Edward Said (1994) picks up on this concept: "Colonial space must be transformed sufficiently so as no longer to appear foreign to the imperial eye" (226). For settlers to feel like the land is theirs, they must familiarize it as they create a space of their own. As they do so, though, they "submerge" Indigenous geographies (Barnd 2017, 10).

Countermapping is a project that intentionally questions traditional Western maps, and as a decolonizing effort, makes Native memory and identity visible and present. This critical spatial practice directly responds to the impacts of settler colonial "smoothing" of landscapes and disrupts the physical presence of settlers. Countermapping is a space-making effort. In Ecuador, for example, Indigenous people use map-making "as a critical tool in their struggles for post-colonial justice" (Radcliffe 2011, 129). The production of maps demonstrates how Indigenous groups can "engage in a politics of struggle against dominant, European-oriented norms of statehood, identity, and knowledge" (129). Basically, these kinds of maps invalidate the absence and invisibility of Native people by creating coded maps that expose the quantity of people that exist and the amount of space that they take up. Once settlers can visualize this information via maps, issues of land rights, assistance, and identity must be acknowledged (133). In this sense, presence equals power. Countermapping seeks to decolonize traditional maps by disrupting what counts as knowledge of land ownership. In the case of Indigenous identity—whether in Ecuador or New Zealand or the United States—simply seeing this information incriminates settler groups. While this concept of decolonizing maps is directly applicable to Indigenous issues, it is likewise applicable to other examples as well. As an act of decolonization, countermapping asserts different ways of reading identity into spatial representation.

Iterations of Countermapping

Maps are not strictly mathematical artifacts but can include "the remembered, the imagined, the contemplated . . . [maps can also] be material or immaterial, actual or desired, whole or part, in various ways experienced, remembered, or projected" (Cosgrove 1999, 2). In this chapter, we identify and analyze three iterations of countermapping: *decolonial artistic*, *anti-lynching persuasive*, and *interactive embodied*. These iterations are intended to show some ways that people have chosen to depict an opposition to dominant views of spatial history and to visually represent information that has either been erased or is simply unknown.

While each type uses different techniques, in some way each communicates a resistance—what Alderman, Inwood, and Bottone (2021) call "oppositional cartographies"—to colonial geographies by opposing dominant views of spatial history or memory and visually representing public inequalities, tragedies, or injustices that have been forgotten or erased (67). Several Indigenous artists engage in decolonial artistic countermapping by using techniques like collage, overlaying, pictographic rendering, and blurring to compel viewers to rethink their perceptions of land ownership, memory, and identity. Interactive embodied countermapping negotiates spatiality by allowing the user to be immersed in the space, and in doing so, brings bodies, emotions, stories, and subjectivities into spaces that have been misidentified, misused, or erased from public memory. Each of the examples we zero in on points back to the overarching endeavor of countermapping as a critical spatial perspective that disrupts racist and colonial forms of spatial representation.

Decolonial Artistic Countermapping

The decolonial artistic countermap mingles art and activism to draw attention to spatial injustices and recount erased narratives. In the examples that we will study, the artists celebrate Native space-making while illustrating the impacts of colonization on Indigenous people. While they focus on Native space-making, it is important to note that decolonial artistic countermapping is not limited to this function but can draw from art and activism to raise awareness about other multiply marginalized and underrepresented communities. According to Natchu Barnd (2017), maps are "both artistic and documentary" because they can perform multiple functions at one time (109). Maps can chronicle the spatialized memory of land, people, and events, but they can also render these concepts in subjective, expressive ways to communicate sociopolitical worldviews. In what follows, we examine the work of Jaune Quick-to-See Smith, Jim Enote, and Ronnie Cachini, but there are many other artists, like Chris Pappan, Terrance Guardipee, and Larson Gasper, who "offer their audiences a visual opportunity to reconsider space, to recognize and restore Native mobilities [as well as] indigenous spatiality—a unique formation of relationship-conscious interaction in the co-constitution of people and place" (109). These artists, who all identify as Native American and are enrolled members in various tribal groups, exemplify the goals of both Indigenous and Black feminist geographies in that they problematize representation and power and make space for public memory that has been whitewashed by dominant cultural narratives. As Dean Rader (2011) asks in his analysis of Quick-to-See Smith's map paintings, "To what degree do the original names for things linger in memory and embodiment? How does one map the invisible?" (49). Rader's questions remind us of the forced invisibility of Native people in the United States and the overarching goal of Indigenous geographies, which asserts the vast number of tribes that still exist throughout the country—in short, they "have neither been vanquished nor have they vanished" (Sasse and Smith 2004, 8).

We define artistic countermapping as a fluid cartographic artifact that can incorporate a range of decorative components, including collage, palimpsest, pictographic, among others. Sometimes artistic countermaps rethink the entire concept of "map," as in the case of Jim Enote and the Zuni artists' series of countermaps of the A:shiwi people. At other times, countermaps begin with a traditional map of the United States and incorporate blurred state lines, Native names, or collages of Western and Native images, as with Jaune Quick-to-See Smith's series of oil and mixed media pieces. It is important that we loosely define these artifacts because each artist approaches the concept of mapping in different ways. Despite the variance in mediums, we would argue that artistic countermaps are what Rader (2011) would call acts of "engaged resistance" (1), which demonstrates the ethical values and strategies of Native artist-activists, including the pursuit of survivance, sovereignty, and autonomy (2). Similarly, artistic countermapping confronts assumptions and stereotypes about Indigenous people through the layering of Western and Native imagery, often in a satirical manner (2–3). While some artistic countermaps intend to shock the viewer, others mean to "bring the viewer in with a seductive texture" (Anreus 1996, 113). Either way, since countermemory is also understood as a rhetoric of resistance, we would argue that artistic countermapping is one way of practicing countermemory.

Jaune Quick-to-See-Smith

In her work, Jaune Quick-to-See Smith presents a subtle yet powerful commentary on land reclamation, broken treaties, name changes, and relocation. At its heart, Quick-to-See Smith's work attends to what Barnd (2017) calls "postcolonial spatial tension" in a way that compels viewers to rethink how they view cartographic public memory in the United States (2). While her oeuvre is vast and diverse, we focus on her various map series, which we would position as artistic countermaps that "centraliz[e] the map as form or container that can be emptied and then refilled" (109). Included in our analysis are four series: "State Names," "Echo Maps," "Tribal Maps," "Browning of America." Quick-to-See Smith, an enrolled member of the Confederated Salish and Kootenai Tribes of the Flathead Nation in Montana, currently resides in New Mexico. Her countermaps are not limited to these geographic regions, though, as she examines large portions of North America, including the United States and Canada. These countermaps use mixed media and oil, and she frequently adds boxes, photos, sticks, and papers to the canvas—what she considers a "'narrative landscape' [that] becomes a map of stories told to fill what has been emptied [by colonization]" (Rader 2011, 51). Her choice of materials is intentional, also, and means to encourage viewers to recognize the "materials, methods, and methodologies of colonization, indigenous histories, and identity" (51).

Echo Maps I, *II*, and *III* utilize a dripping technique, which smears state and national borders and blurs the layered images on the canvas. Also apparent on *I* and *II* are variations of the word "Hello" in Spanish and other languages, especially *hola* and *allo*, and clippings from global newspapers within the state boundaries. Quick-to-See Smith focuses on the relationship between language and land in this series and reminds her viewers that the United States is a diverse country where multiple languages are spoken, which is a direct rebuttal to white nationalism's cry for a country of white, English-speaking residents. Since Spanish is one of the dominant languages represented in these countermaps, Quick-to-See-Smith also presents a commentary about the significance of Latinx sociocultural influences not just at the border of the United States and Mexico but around the nation. This series of countermaps contains many different types of echoes, including the repetition of greetings (*Hola*, *Allo*, and *Nin hao*), newspaper articles, advertisements, and other images. The repetition indicates that language is in flux, as are the people who speak these languages. In *Echo II*, the Chinese greeting *Nin hao* is scattered throughout North America and Cuba, which reminds the viewer that state and national boundaries have no bearing on language—it continues to move, evolve, and impact both people and land. Rader (2011) also notes the impact of the aural/visual connection in these countermaps: "Smith's maps use their visuality as an aural reminder that voices do not exist in a vacuum; language is concatenated by repetition and renewal" (58). Through the echoes of languages and images, Quick-to-See Smith again disrupts the objectivity of the map; by re/imagining the traditional US map through these repetitions, she causes the viewer to question the ownership of land and the composition of these spaces and places.

In her *Tribal Map* series of two paintings, Quick-to-See Smith again integrates the whitewashing technique while making a more overt argument about land ownerships and Indigenous autonomy. Nowhere on either *Tribal I* or *II* does the viewer see Anglo versions of state or national names; in their place are tribal names. While she maintains the traditional US map with its borders intact, she jars the viewers with the absence of state names and the inclusion of tribal names. These countermaps ask viewers to consider the colonizing reality of land-naming and make visible the Native tribes that have been erased from memory. Zuni countermapper Jim Enote explains that most maps "completely leave off the meaning of the place," and in doing so, "replac[es] Native language . . . with something that is not really from here." Quick-to-See Smith's *Tribal Map* series revives Native meaning; she creates spaces by renaming those that have been overwritten by colonization and displacement. However, by still maintaining state and national boundaries that are familiar to non-Native viewers, Quick-to-See Smith quietly persuades, which is consistent with her artistic vision to seduce her audience with her worldview. Barnd (2017) writes, "In many ways, her impressionistic interpretation intentionally increases the invisibility of some elements of the standard map. She consciously uses the 'seduction' technique—what she also refers to as a 'sneak up'—that encourages her viewers to look closer and then 'reach a level of understanding that her messages have serious implications'" (110). The map is just familiar enough to draw the viewer into deeper introspection of the tribal names that overwrite state names.

In her last countermapping series, *Browning of America*, we see a slight shift in Quick-to-See Smith's work. Some elements remain the same, including a clear demarcation of national boundaries, the layering of text, and the paint dripping down the canvas in long streams. However, Quick-to-See Smith uses a reddish-brown paint instead of white paint to drip and smear the canvas; the effect is an antiqued appearance. She also paints petroglyphs throughout the canvas, including an armless human across the border of New Mexico, Texas, and Mexico; a human with long, wavy arms who straddles Louisiana, Mississippi, and Alabama; and various mammals in the Midwest, Mexico, and the Gulf of Mexico. In *Browning II*, the list of "Invaders from the East" is more clearly visible and lists colonizing groups over a thousand-year timeline as a "sidebar" to the focus of Indigenous memory, which dominates the canvas (Barnd 2017, 112). These petroglyphs, along with the lack of clear state boundaries, demonstrate Native space-making—the petroglyphs "inhabit and imbue land [and also] inscribe the reality that space is lived" (Rader 2011, 68). Quick-to-See Smith's countermapping enacts the primary goals of Indigenous geographies, namely, to demonstrate how Native people make space, to re-narrate place, and to confront settler-colonialism (Barnd 2017, 1–2). She accomplishes these purposes by employing artistic and mapping practices to resist dominant narratives about Native people, including the attempts to make Native memory, identity, and land ownership invisible.

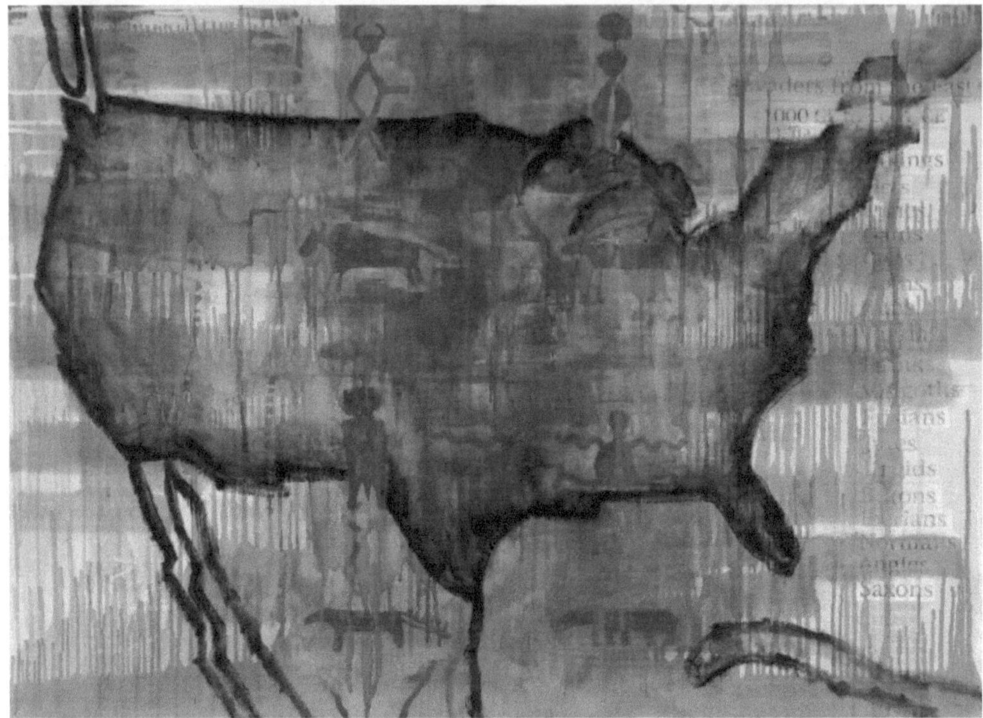

Figure 12. "Browning in America" by artist Jaune Quick-to-See Smith, 2020.

Quick-to-See-Smith's countermaps resist any boundaries and seek to communicate broader messages about Native sovereignty through a genre that appears familiar to her viewers. The power of the familiar is that it allows viewers to question what has previously been taught (perhaps in the classroom or via public memory sources) and to reimagine Native space. Barnd (2017) argues that Quick-to-See Smith's maps open up discussion about land ownership, Native identity, and settler colonialism: "In her capable hands, the US map becomes an entry point for cultural, historic, and political engagement. It becomes an interrogation of space, of the ways we construct and sustain spatialities and of the fact that they too exist in layers. Maps become documents of what existed in the past, but also what now exists, and how we know about these existences and transitions" (111). Artistic countermaps work with a person's capacity to determine where things are in relation to each other, and in the case of Quick-to-See Smith, she challenges the viewer's mental mapping with a Native-centered approach.

Jim Enote and A:shiwi Artists

Jim Enote, a traditional Zuni farmer in New Mexico, also directs the A:shiwi A:wan Museum and Heritage Center, a "Pueblo of Zuni Tribal Program dedicated to serving the Zuni community with programs and exhibitions that help us reflect on our past and are relevant to our current and future interests" ("About the Museum," n.d.). The museum and center emphasizes A:shiwi ways of knowing alongside modern concepts of knowledge. One of its most expansive exhibits is the *A:shiwi A:wan Ulohnanne—The Zuni World*, which is a series of countermaps depicting the land of the A:shiwi. These countermaps, created by Zuni artists, elders, and council members, seek to "reclaim the names of Zuni places and depict the land of the A:shiwi as they know and see it . . . with culture, story, and prayer . . . [because] modern maps do not have a memory" (Loften and Vaughan-Lee 2019). Enote contrasts traditional Western maps with the Zuni countermaps: whereas Google maps help people navigate from one place to another, they omit the meaning of the place. Because conventional maps in New Mexico (and elsewhere in the United States) are typically formatted for English or Spanish, they, in effect, replace and eclipse Zuni language and knowledge. Enote argues, "This whole constellation of what makes up a map is far beyond a piece of paper" (Loften and Vaughan-Lee 2019). Thus, the Zuni countermaps are composed of colorful, textured images, stories, and prayer. As Enote explains, he wanted to make maps that were "elegant, evocative, and profoundly important to the Zuni people" (Loften and Vaughan-Lee 2019). As a result, these maps do not look like traditional maps or atlases, yet take a different perspective than the countermaps crafted by more mainstream Indigenous artists.

Jake Skeets (2020), a Navajo writer, explains how the work of Indigenous artists and authors is one that seeks a "radical remembering." "In a way, I am arguing for the recategorizing of land through radical remembering and the memory field [. . .] Through radical remembering we are able to reclaim these wilds and frontiers as intimate parts of our very being. In that way, wilds and frontiers are transformed into homes and fields. They become part of the domestic, the intimate, and the spiritual. By reclaiming memory as a thing we can touch, we give a body to the memory machine that exists inside of our minds. It is this body that tells us stories. This body, our body, tells us stories. And sometimes our body listens for us to tell the stories of ponds, windmills, downtown buildings, apartment kitchens, dining tables, and tadpoles. We remember them and continue to remember them."

Figure 13. "Sights in the Grand Canyon" by artist Ronnie Cachini, 2010.

The A:shiwi countermaps are not intended for a white audience; rather, they are intended for an A:shiwi audience. One of the Zuni artists, Ronnie Cachini, focuses on conveying the significant places that only a Zuni would know. Cachini, who is also a medicine man for the Eagle Plume Down Medicine Society and head rain priest, resists the notion that maps can represent "Truth" and objectivity and seeks to expose the elements that conventional maps conceal, including where we are from or who we are. His countermaps teach observers to "listen to the land around us" as we search for the memory that has been erased by dominant cultural narratives. His *Sites in the Grand Canyon* was inspired by a large boulder covered with petroglyphs. Upon studying the petroglyphs, Cachini realized that the boulder was actually a map of the Colorado River, and each petroglyph depicted a place, a story, or a prayer. He designed *Sites of the Grand Canyon* to mirror the map on the boulder: the base layer is a rich brown color and depicts the petroglyphs. In place of many of the petroglyphs, Cachini painted the various places they represent, including side canyons, rivers, and burial sites. As already suggested, unlike some of the more mainstream countermaps, the Zuni maps often tie in prayers, functioning to remember traditional Zuni prayers, which again brings a sense of reverence for the land and the people who have lived there before white men colonized the spaces and places. Cachini explains that the purpose behind the countermap is for the A:shiwi to "never let [themselves] go . . . never forgetting who you are, where you came from" (Loften and Vaughan-Lee 2019). Cachini's exhortation—to hold on to cultural memory—is echoed throughout the artistic countermaps that we have examined. While Quick-to-See Smith, Cachini, and others accomplish this goal in various ways, each of the artistic countermaps here rejects the settler colonial narrative and highlights Indigenous presence, both historically and in contemporary life. The relationship between mapping and storytelling is undeniable, and the use of these countermaps acknowledges that there are many types of knowledge.

Anti-Lynching Persuasive Countermapping

According to Alderman, Inwood, and Bottone (2021), this genre of mapping is composed of two sparts: anti-lynching campaigning and persuasive mapping (71). One of the main objectives of anti-lynching campaigns is to collect, tabulate, interpret, visualize, and publicize data regarding the murder of Black individuals, in order to shift national conversations and promote legal reparations for these actions. Likewise, persuasive mapping, a term coined by Judith Tyner (2020), seeks to "shape public opinion and gain the support of elected officials" (71). Joining these two aspects together, anti-lynching persuasive countermaps seek to use data to persuade the public that lynching is local, both in its historical examples and in contemporary practices via police violence. What we mean by this is that we cannot disassociate ourselves from anti-Black violence, whether by arguing that lynching was something that happened a long time ago or by arguing that it did not occur anywhere except the Deep South.

Alderman, Inwood, and Bottone (2021) examine a range of anti-lynching persuasive countermaps, including some collected by the NAACP for the period 1889 to 1919 (NAACP 1919). One example of such a countermap focuses on 1909–1918, using a simple black and white, cross-hatching design (fig. 14). Each state is labeled, and for states with a relatively small number of lynchings, an "x" illustrates how many individuals were killed in that period. For states with greater numbers, the NAACP countermappers drew lines across the state. The closer the lines, the more lynchings occurred in that state. For those states with the largest number of lynchings, including Texas, Louisiana, Mississippi, Georgia, and Florida, the state is completely colored black. The effect of this simple data visualization is that someone with no frame of reference can quickly glimpse at the countermap and understand the information being communicated. First, we learn that the largest number of lynchings occurred in Texas and the Deep South, but we also learn that lynchings occurred in northern states as well. This countermap demonstrates the goal of early anti-lynching persuasive countermaps—these cartographers believed that the data itself was persuasive, especially in conjunction with the book it was published in, which chronicles all the individual victims' names and the dates of the violence against them.

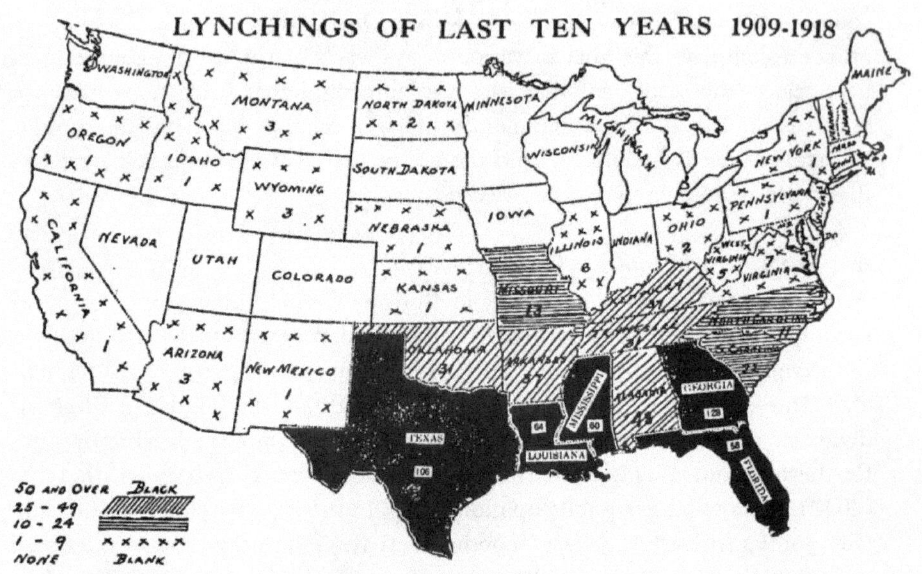

Figure 14. Map of lynchings between 1909 and 1918. From *Thirty Years of Lynching in the United States, 1889–1918*; Library of Congress.

Similar to the NAACP, the Tuskegee Institute Research Development created a countermap that visualized lynching data—but at the state and county level. In their case, the countermap appears alongside tabular data. The Tuskegee countermap uses dots to represent each lynching, so the effect when viewed from afar is a darkening of dots as they merge in the places where lynchings were more prevalent. Their data also supports the information from the NAACP countermap, with the largest number of lynchings between East Texas at the western boundary and the Georgia coastline at the eastern boundary. Still, again like the NAACP map, is the Tuskegee map provides evidence of lynchings all over the United States.

As Alderman, Inwood, and Bottone (2021) point out, though, these countermaps belie the challenges that these cartographies encountered. One of the most significant challenges was verifying the exact location of the lynching—over 15 percent of reported lynchings cannot be traced to any specific location

(72). Compounding these challenges were forces that actively combatted efforts to communicate this lynching information. Often, lynchings were dubbed "race riots," or just instances of white mob violence. Alderman, Inwood, and Bottone argue that these issues demonstrate a larger problem of power and knowledge: Specifically, who gets to decide what information is released to the public? They write, "The Tuskegee map reminds us of the challenges of mapping against the power structures responsible for the lynching and dislocation of Black life; those racist structures can obfuscate efforts to reconstruct the injustice" (72). Tuskegee's countermap exhibits the challenges of spatializing the countermemory of lynching—in many cases, the information is just not there, or it is purposely obscured.

In addition to these more historic examples are some more recent projects that seek to raise awareness about the erased memory of lynchings. Among them are the sweeping *Lynching in America* project from the Equal Justice Initiative (EJI), which includes maps—including interactive ones—that illustrate events surrounding anti-Black lynching acts, among them *The Great Migration* and *Racial Terror Lynchings* maps. *Racial Terror Lynchings* visualizes the data from the EJI's comprehensive examination of the 4,440 individuals who were lynched between 1877–1950. While many more people were lynched, these were the documented cases that the EJI uncovered in their research. Like the other anti-lynching persuasive countermaps, *Racial Terror Lynchings* actively resists the dominant cultural narrative that seeks to erase the memory of these individuals, and it also presents facts and data. The user can hover over each state to see the number of people who were lynched, and the map, which is mostly in dark colors, lights up in red with the number listed. The simple key on the bottom right of the screen shows that states with the least number of lynchings are in black and states with the most number are in red. Along with the number of people who were lynched, the *Racial Terror Lynchings* countermap also incorporates information about specific people. For example, when a user hovers over a white dot in East Texas, an informational bubble appears with the name of Henry Smith, a man who was lynched in Lamar County. When the user clicks on the informational bubble, a short video plays with footage from Smith's murder and a voiceover that explains how he was lynched and informs the viewer that there is no marker placed to remember this event. The EJI's countermap leverages multimodal elements like images, videos, voice, sound, and text to persuade the viewer of the horrors of racial terror lynchings and the need for action.

Similar to the *Racial Terror Lynchings* countermap, *Lynching in Texas* is an interactive map, one that focuses specifically on lynchings in Texas and provides archival research for each listing. The countermap, created by historian Jeff Littlejohn and several students, allows users to zoom in and out. When zoomed out, the countermap displays a colored circle with a number representing the lynchings in each of the main regions in Texas, including 33 lynchings in West Texas, 20 in the Texas panhandle, 135 in northeast Texas, 398 in East Texas, and 150 in South Texas. Through only a cursory inspection, the countermap illustrates the fact that most lynchings in Texas occurred in the eastern half of the state. As part of the countermap's interactivity, users can click on each of the larger colored bubbles, which then break down into smaller bubbles with a specific number of lynchings. Each time the user clicks on a bubble, the number of bubbles becomes greater, and the user zooms further and further on a specific region. Once users zoom into a single lynching and click on the bubble, the name of the person who was lynched appears, along with a thumbnail of a newspaper clipping.

After the user clicks on the thumbnail, the archival research appears on the screen. For each case, *Lynching in Texas* provides the name of the person, the date they were lynched, other identifying information, and (at the bottom of the screen), any archival information has been linked to that person. This information usually takes the form of newspaper clippings that illustrate the callousness with which the lynching victims were treated. As a whole, *Lynching in Texas* demonstrates several aspects of the anti-lynching persuasive countermap: like its counterparts, the map shows data, along with archival research to communicate information to users. It persuades through logos. What makes this countermap particularly effective, though, is its interactivity at the local level. When students in April O'Brien's "Public Memory and Countermemory" course examined the *Lynching in Texas* countermap for a weekly assignment, they were struck by how many people were lynched near their hometowns. As they gained that sense of geographic knowledge, they were dismayed at never learning this information at school prior to taking April's course. Their responses highlight the importance of countermapping at the local level, through which more people could be educated about the injustices in American history.

Interactive Embodied Countermapping

The third type of countermap, the interactive embodied genre, "releases cartography from its bonds of convention" (Alderman, Inwood, and Bottone 2021, 76) by bringing bodies, materiality, and affect into conversation with map-making efforts. As geographers Rob Kitchin, Justin Gleeson, and Martin Dodge (2013) explain, scholars are beginning to move from creating/critiquing maps within an ontological framework to an ontogenetic one. This shift in focus alters the primary question from what things *are* to how things *become* (494). Furthermore, Kitchin, Gleeson, and Dodge argue that as we shift from a "scientific" notion of mapping to a "processual" approach that considers the process and meaning behind map-making, we can recognize that maps are ecological and constantly in a state of flux (see also Edbauer 2009, 9). While many of the countermaps that we have analyzed in this chapter defy traditional cartographic principles, the interactive embodied countermap completely rethinks the boundaries of cartography. These maps are characterized by their interactivity, which encourages viewers and visitors to become a part of the experience. This interactivity can be achieved digitally, via an immersive virtual reality (VR) interface, as well as by physically moving through a space. Whether experienced digitally or in person, interactive embodied countermaps anticipate and encourage human interaction. As a result, they tend to elicit an affective response by compelling visitors to acknowledge and take responsibility for erased memories that have been suppressed by dominant cultural narratives. Likewise, the role of the material cannot be overstated with regard to these countermaps. Each has an inherent materiality that is tied to its meaning and impact.

We begin the analysis here with the NMPJ, the lynching memorial sponsored by the EJI. This memorial (fig. 15), which "maps" some of the individuals who were lynched between 1877 and 1950, is part of the EJI's comprehensive goal to inspire an "era of truth-telling about racial injustice" (EJI 2021, 119). NMPJ is also an example of countermapping: while not composed within the traditional confines of cartography, the memorial nonetheless takes visitors through a journey that maps the names of those who were lynched, along with state and county-level information relevant to the specific case and the date of the murder.

Figure 15. Hanging steel monuments at the National Memorial for Peace and Justice engraved with the names, dates, and locations of individuals who were lynched; photograph by April O'Brien.

The NMPJ's steel monuments, suspended from the ceiling, allude to the method by which many Black Americans were hung from trees. The steel monuments are organized according to states and counties; thus, a visitor can walk in a straight line to view the section for South Carolina, Texas, Virginia, or any other state. The experience functions like a map, but a far more embodied mapping experience than simply looking at a map on a wall. The body's moving through the NMPJ is similar to tracing the boundaries, state names, and other aspects of a physical map. For example, when April visited the memorial, she was most concerned about lynchings in South Carolina, so she approached the sites as she would approach a map. When reading a map, users often access the key or start with a familiar location and trace the information from that vantage point. Similarly, when "reading" the NMPJ as a map, April studied the organization of the steel monuments and first realized that they were organized in alphabetical order according to state. Once she found the state she was looking for, though, she could easily move through the space in a straight line to study South Carolina monuments, organized in alphabetical order for each county.

While the NMPJ serves as one iteration of an interactive embodied countermap, the next example depicts how VR can be leveraged for this genre as well. In "Mapping and/as Remembering," O'Brien (2020b) describes a VR countermap project in Pendleton, South Carolina (fig. 16). This project, which she collaboratively composed with community members, used "punctum to map erased memory sites." Punctum, a term used by Roland Barthes, "can be understood as anything seen, heard, felt, or experienced that pierces one's consciousness" (O'Brien 2020b). In this case, O'Brien describes being haunted by the absence of truth-telling in the town's public memory and its refusal to address the role of slavery in the town's formation or the impact of racial terror, Jim Crow laws, and segregation on the town's development. Working with the Pendleton Foundation for Black History and Culture, she collected oral histories and archival information, a process that educated her about various details that were not communicated by the town's historical foundation. Some of this information included details about lynchings, fear of violence from white residents if Black residents left the west side of town, the role of the NAACP in fighting for civil rights during integration, and several Black entrepreneurs. The disparity between Pendleton's public memory and these stories was vast; it was nothing short of complete erasure of Black history in the town. As with the other types of countermaps we have discussed in this chapter, the VR countermap was a response to dominant cultural memory, which refuses all truth-telling efforts and suppresses any memories that diverge from the accepted view of history that centers white men.

Similar to the NMPJ, the VR project, which is called *Counter-Tour: Remembering Black History in Pendleton, South Carolina*, expands our understanding

Figure 16. Screenshot of *Counter-Tour: Remembering Black History in Pendleton, South Carolina*; created by April O'Brien.

of cartography in that it incorporates more interactivity and embodiment. As Alderman, Inwood, and Bottone (2021) argue, by "restricting cartographic to a narrow academic understanding forecloses the geospatial significance of [. . .] activism" (74). *Counter-Tour* does not fit within the parameters of a conventional map, but like the NMPJ, still functions to tell a spatialized story. Likewise, *Counter-Tour* is an artifact of activism; it responds to the purposeful gaps in public history in Pendleton and forces people to a reckoning of racial violence and inequalities that existed in the past and persist within the town. It does so through a series of VR images that flow into each other. For example, the map begins at the center of town on the Village Green. Users can click on informational bubbles within that space or click on a bubble that takes them in various directions that branch off from the center of town. The end result is a completely interactive maplike experience, where users can spatially experience the town. Unlike a traditional map, though, this countermap educates users about the gaps in Pendleton's public memory and functions as a truth-telling apparatus. Relying on the oral histories April collected, each space on the countermap teaches users about the stories and experiences that have been erased by dominant cultural narratives.

In addition to these interactive components, *Counter-Tour* is also embodied in a couple of different capacities. First, this type of countermap encourages bodies to engage with the content. The act of scrolling on the page and clicking the mouse immediately engages various senses. Since the countermap is created with Thinglink, users can incorporate Microsoft's Immersive Reader, so that text descriptions, lessons, virtual tours, infographics, and videos are all accessible. Secondly, *Counter-Tour* projects the Black bodies, lives, and communities that have been impacted by racism in Pendleton. As McKittrick and Woods (2007) remind us, "Black places, experiences, histories, and people that no one knows do exist within our present geographic order" (4). In other words, as users (particularly users who live in the Pendleton area or are familiar with the landscape) engage with the countermap in all the spaces and places, they are able to see the stories that have been erased and how they are superimposed on top of the places that they know well. "No one knows?" Yes, by all accounts, no one knows many of the Black histories in the United States because they have been deleted from public memory. The work of countermemory is to recover what has been erased, and countermaps allow people to leverage geography for these purposes. Where "bodies, emotions, and subjectivities have been [removed] from traditional framings of geospatial technologies," countermaps redress these inequalities, these absences, and promote a more socially just cartographic practice (Kwan 2007, 30).

Conclusion

While Indigenous countermaps emphasize survivance and sovereignty and Black countermaps underscore the violence of racial terror lynching, both serve as reminders of the ways in which whitestream American public memory seeks to erase these stories from public record. In each case, Indigenous and Black countermappers hold a mirror up to American culture and insist that we all see. As Indigenous activists remind white colonizers again and again: *We are still here*. Likewise, these countermaps insist that these events occurred, these people lived, and to move forward in any capacity, we must begin by visualizing these memories via countermapping. Thinking in terms of absences and presences, liberatory countermaps take memories, spaces, and truths that many Americans wish to not remember—or might not even know—and give them literal and metaphorical space to exist. Countermappers hold the power to make the unknown know and can construct the material artifact that moves an absence to a presence. This garners a creator-maker ethos that we further discuss through popular culture mediums in the next chapter.

Mapmaking is a critical tool used to promote truth-telling efforts, to fight for postcolonial justice, and to make visible that which has been erased from public memory (Radcliffe 2011, 129). Countermaps can declare subaltern presence, as with many of the decolonial artistic maps, or they can communicate data and facts about lynching and continuing racialized violence against Black individuals. Countermaps can even defy conventional cartographic principles, as with interactive embodied maps. As Crampton and Krygier (2005) contend, "maps are active; they actively construct knowledge, they exercise power, and they can be a powerful means of promoting social change" (15). Since countermapping is a method to enact a rhetoric of countermemory, the act itself is a practice that is particularly active, naturally constructs and communicates new knowledge, and inspires social change.

Each of the iterations of countermapping we analyzed illustrates the various ways that artists, scholars, and activists enact a disruption of racist and colonial forms of spatial representation. Whether we study Quick-to-See-Smith's *Browning of America*, visit the NMPJ, or experience a small town's Black history via VR, we encounter similar threads of resistance. Countermapping as a theory and practice finds new ways to oppose white, American exceptionalist views of space and place; it likewise opens our awareness to visual representations of public inequalities, tragedies, and injustices. This work is vital, especially as we experience attacks against truth-telling efforts each day in many state legislatures. The exigency of countermapping is undeniable, even as school boards across Texas fight for so-called transparency in education, which in practice includes banning books and conversations about the United States' legacy of racism and injustice. While countermapping cannot alone combat the surge in anti-CRT laws and the loss of academic freedom in higher education, these artifacts can provide awareness and start conversations in a highly volatile sociopolitical climate.

3

"I Am America's Son"

The Counterappropriation of White Supremacy Narratives in Popular Culture

In 2020, a white supremacist group, the Proud Boys, made headlines after then-president Trump decided to not denounce them while in a debate with Joe Biden, instead telling the hate organization to "stand back and stand by." Some conservative talking heads downplayed Trump's remarks because he said he "would" denounce them, but in reality, many white supremacists, including the Proud Boys, took Trump's call "seriously and literally" (Krakauer 2023; Zito 2016). A few of them tweeted during and after the debate to say they were ready to stand with Trump whenever he needed them, using the hashtag #ProudBoys to spread their messages. Most of the uses of the hashtag right after Trump's debate pronouncement promoted pro-Proud Boy messages, though a few dissenters did use the tag to criticize the organization.

However, the permutations of the hashtag quickly evolved after the debate. Actor and LGBTQ activist George Takei (2020) tweeted, "I wonder if the BTS [a popular Korean band] and TikTok kids can help LGBTs with this. What if gay guys took pictures of themselves making out with each other or doing very gay things, then tagged themselves with #ProudBoys. I bet it would mess them up real bad. #ReclaimingMyShine." Soon after, the hashtag #ProudBoys proliferated with photos of people demonstrating gay pride. Actors, activists, and other Twitter users, posted photos of their gay pride—typically with two people presenting as men kissing or being affectionate with a male-facing individual. BBC found an uptick in the hashtag usage, claiming "#ProudBoys" had been tweeted eighty-eight thousand times in less than a week after the debate ("Proud Boys" 2020).

Rhetorically, Takei's call and the subsequent Twitter flood appropriated the hashtag white supremacists utilized to organize or spread their ideologies and flipped it in order to counteract the racism. The tag could no longer fully represent the vernacular symbols of white supremacists—it fluctuated to signify the pride of gay men, in an obvious antithesis to the ideology of the Proud Boys. Symbolic language and messages like this alter constantly, from being either apolitical or positive one moment to flipping to a negative or bigoted cause the next. For instance, Pepe the Frog, a benign, awkward online meme, was appropriated by white supremacists during Trump's election in 2016, and the creator of the image and others are currently fighting legal battles to reappropriate it back to its original, happy-go-lucky iteration (see Jones 2020 for a more detailed account). The malleable nature of these symbols means that anything could change from time to time for a multitude of reasons, based upon a community's or public's objectives. Yet, this appropriation process plays out not only in the symbols or memes that people use but also in our popular culture narratives.

Different groups have appropriated multitudes of symbols and narratives for their own collective purposes, historically speaking, some for political reasons, some for reasons related to sovereignty, some for the memes, and others for critique. This chapter focuses on a specific type of appropriation, though, what we might call "counterappropriation," looking specifically at symbols and narratives often associated with white supremacists and how, reflecting our broader analysis of liberatory countermemories, others attempt to diminish their original hateful charge via the appropriation act. The acts we examine exist in various forms of popular culture—TV shows, music, and art. Specifically, we analyze Damon Lindelof's limited TV series *Watchmen*; Childish Gambino's song and music video "This Is America"; Gary Clark Jr.'s song and music video "This Land"; and Ken Gonzales-Day's art installation *Erased Lynchings* (2006). Each of these pieces of popular culture—in different symbolic gestures and utterances—attempts to counterappropriate some form of white supremacy and thus works as an extension of countermemory.

Overall, these artists employ counterappropriation to make provocative statements about racist history: moving from critiques of racism in the comic book industry to arguments about racist violence in contemporary America, from appropriating the history of Confederate memorabilia to appropriating lynching photography. In these specific artifacts, the artists use racist narratives, symbols, and iconography to help audiences rewrite a shared understanding of America's past. The counterappropriations are a specific *method* artists use to illustrate undertold and underreported histories within an anti-racist framework. Therefore, the symbolism becomes the method of distributing anti-racist countermemory.

Counterappropriation as Countermemory

In his article "The Rhetoric of Intertextuality" (2010), Frank J. D'Angelo breaks down the various types of intertextual (rhetorical) moves people can make in any given discursive act, which, of course, includes appropriation. He cites Marita Sturken and Lisa Cartwright (2001), who define appropriation as "the act of borrowing, stealing, or taking over others' meanings to one's own ends" (36). D'Angelo's analysis stems from an art perspective—framing appropriation as it relates to plagiarism (Sartwell 1998), postmodern photography, and copyright issues (Phares 1998). He focuses on the appropriation of ideas rather than of symbols. Similarly, in *The Culture of Copy*, Hillel Schwartz (1996) refers to appropriation—discussing visual culture in the 1980s—as "copying is assimilation, reenactment is appropriation, appropriation is creation" (246). To Schwartz, the iterative formations of copying and reenacting provide a space for new meaning to emerge. Though much of the analysis of appropriation as a rhetorical act stems from artists appropriating other artists, we expand the concept to consider how "artists" (in the broadest sense of the term) appropriate not "art" per se but symbols of white supremacy. In this chapter, we are not talking about "copying" or "reenacting" as generative acts. None of the artists we analyze solely do one or the other—most of them appropriate symbols, narratives, or ideas, things that could not be easily tied to copyright or singular owners.

Nonetheless, these individuals still appropriate as a means to create. The purpose of these appropriations is not to steal someone's idea for art, but rather, to say "fuck you" to white supremacy. The appropriations alter the power dynamics of racism. By taking historical narratives of oppression (as in *Watchmen*), symbols of white supremacy and the Confederacy (as in music videos by Childish Gambino and Gary Clark Jr.), and images of historical lynchings (as with Ken Gonzales-Day's art installation), these various artists appropriate the history of white terror and racism to show demonstrate that they have the power and platform to belittle them openly and publicly. Though their art does not literally refashion the bigoted dynamics at play, it openly challenges them. These artists allow room for people to participate in the challenging and belittling act against white supremacy. Their appropriation exists as an invitation to critique racism on an intellectual level but also mock it in what we will call "counterappropriation."

This type of rhetorical practice is not new, however. In her article "Counterhegemonic Acts: Appropriation as a Feminist Rhetorical Strategy," Helene A. Shugart (1997) defines the practice of counterappropriation as follows: "A popular strategy of members of various disenfranchised social groups is to claim and utilize labels conventionally applied by their oppressions in a derogatory manner as a way to challenge their original meaning. Some lesbians and gay men, for example, refer to themselves as dykes or faggots, respectively some African Americans defiantly refer to themselves as [the 'n-word']; and some women celebrate their identities as whores and bitches" (210). Shugart examines how disenfranchised groups often appropriate derogatory terms used against them as a way to empower themselves and also steal power away from incendiary language users. Before going into her analysis of feminist counterhegemonic acts, she explores how theorists have defined the (in)effectiveness of submerged people appropriating "oppressive paradigms" in the past. She finds that some theorists reject such appropriation because they find it to still be exploitative (Johnson 1990) or that it reaffirms the status of the oppressor (Bammer 1982). However, others like Cixous (1976), view this type of appropriation as "actional and assertive and thus revolutionary" (213). Shugart (1997) illustrates how the efficacy of this act divides critics, concluding that "subversive appropriation is a highly complex enterprise, reflective of the equally complex issues of power, ideology, and hegemony with which it deals" (226). Furthermore, there are multiple types of these appropriations that exist outside of feminist discourse, which makes subversive appropriation an effective strategy.

Still, the artifacts examined in this chapter use appropriation a bit differently than how Shugart employs counterappropriation. For our purposes, we identify ways to take symbols and narratives of the oppressor and patronize them, rather than appropriating a term or message to demean the oppressed. Doing so flips the script on power dynamics. Theorists often write about reclaiming territory or space that is yours via appropriation, an empowering tactic, but what happens when you claim the oppressor's territory? These cases in this chapter do not suggest that certain hurtful narratives can be redirected as empowerment; rather, they take what the oppressor deems important—symbols of the Confederacy, narratives of KKK and hyperviolence, and lynching photographs—and strip away their meaning and purpose via the appropriation act. While the artifacts and narratives still contain elements and charges of degradation, such as symbols of the Confederacy, the way these symbols are applied are not to claim power via belittling others. Rather, often, these are artifacts that constitute white supremacy collectives. The Confederate flag, history of the Klan, and hyperviolence against people of color all exist as means to develop community for white supremacists, a way to differentiate themselves from people of color. Similarly, while the lynching photographs do depict overt subjugation, they only became popular because they were postcards that white people shared with one another, marking them as relational and transactional performance. Therefore, the appropriations analyzed in this chapter are meant to strip white people of their supremacist power, lampooning and disparaging the symbols that comprise their collective identity.

Liberatory counterappropriation, therefore, is an extension of countermemory. It does not focus as much on overt history and memory claims as other categories of countermemory, such as occurs with statues, memorials, and maps, but it performs countermemory through the appropriation act. By taking a symbol of white supremacy and altering its symbolic history, these artists and activists asks audiences to reengage with what that history is, what it means to change it, and how ridiculing white supremacy can alter the way people interact with it in the future. Counterappropriation emphasizes the mechanisms that allow bigotry to flourish and uses the history of these symbols as the means to challenge them. So, while its function is not necessarily the same (countermemory focuses more on challenging history/memory while counterappropriation focuses more on challenging symbols), it still attempts to alter history—not historical moments, people, or themes but the uses of certain narratives and representations in the present. Counterappropriation changes how we interact with overarching narratives.

Watchmen as a Retelling of the History of Racism

The opening of Damon Lindelof's hit limited series *Watchmen* (2019) does not begin with the Tulsa Race Massacre, though if you had read Twitter soon after the premiere or reviews online that is what you would have been led to believe. The massacre actually starts around the 2:00 mark in the episode; before this, audiences watch a rendition of a black-and-white, early twentieth-century film. In this "old" movie, a white man (playing the archetype of a "bandit") dressed in all white shoots at a vigilante, donned in full black garb, on a dark horse. The man in full black attempts to rope the man in white off his horse. This occurs outside of a church. A priest then steps out and questions the vigilante, asking why he is hurting the (revealed) sheriff, after which the vigilante pulls back his hood to illustrate he's a Black man—"the Black Marshal of Oklahoma [Bass Reeves]!" The churchgoers want to lynch the white sheriff for his crimes, but the Black marshal says we should "trust in the law." The TV show then cuts to a young Black boy who watches—and recites—the film while his mother plays the piano for an empty theater and sheds a single tear. From there, the infamous racist bombing of Tulsa begins, starting right outside of the theater.

This short scene to open the series is a bit convoluted but powerful, nonetheless. Though we do not know the title of the black-and-white film or if the film is for all audiences or just for Black audiences—as a mean to instill hope and justice for the oppressed community—it does not matter, because Lindelof expresses the thematic core of the entire show in this opening cold open for the actual audience of 2019: the counterappropriation of white supremacy. Some audiences may not understand it, but a keen audience would notice the parallels between this short film and D. W. Griffith's infamous film *The Birth of a Nation* (1915). Griffith's film depicts the Ku Klux Klan as the guardians of American culture and values. In one of its most racist moments, Gus, a Black freedman, pursues a white woman who jumps off a cliff because she would rather die than be raped by him. The Klan, with their white rage, hunt down Gus and lynch him for causing the white woman's death. Griffith's film is often cited as one of the first films taken seriously in American cinema and was the first film viewed in the White House, by then-president Woodrow Wilson. It is also historically situated as one the most racist films in American cinema.

Thus, Lindelof takes Griffith's trope of the Klan lynching the Black man for unwanted sexual advances and reappropriates it in the very opening of his series. Audiences are meant to be a bit confused or feel disjointed by the sequence since we never see a Black man wearing all-black clothing be the hero of the story over a white sheriff who is dressed in all-white attire. Lindelof's twist embodies the pro-Black, antiracist theme central to the show's narrative; yet it also works to dismantle pro-white tropes that are uncritically tied to our memory of the past.

If the collective memory of vigilantism in the United States is that of the white savior, then the opening of *Watchmen* exists to counter that historical narrative. Whereas other countermemories or counternarratives exist to challenge actual history, *Watchmen*'s narrative differs because it is set in a fictional universe. Instead of promoting a different view of history or recovering something erased from the record, Lindelof takes the route of simply challenging a trope, one deemed unequivocally racist. In some sense, this approach moves past history and focuses on epistemology—the ways people see, interact, and make knowledge in our world via these tropes. Yet, while countering a long, racist narrative, Lindelof's opening also successfully juxtaposes the racial utopia expressed on the screen with the reality of the Tulsa Race Massacre that subsequently follows it. While we can live in the world of Blackness-as-goodness in the cinema and can challenge our predispositions, the truth exists in the reality of that fictional universe, where the race massacre that experts believe killed hundreds of Black people and injured hundreds more persists. We can challenge history. We can promote new narratives. But at the end of the day, our pasts—even in fictional worlds—are still our realities.

Lindelof's limited series peaks its counterappropriation narrative in episode 6, "This Extraordinary Being." The episode begins with Hooded Justice, the most mysterious character in the original *Watchmen* universe (Chin), being interrogated by two detectives. The original *Watchmen* comic series occurs in the mid-1980s, in a fictional universe that mirrors our own, where we are on the brink of nuclear war with the Soviet Union. Masked vigilantes (only one character with true "superpowers," Dr. Manhattan) have been fighting crimes in the city for decades but have recently been outlawed. In 1985, the vigilantes converge to stop the murders of other vigilantes and prevent war between the United States and Soviet Union. Yet these are not the only vigilantes that exist in this universe.

Hooded Justice was one of the first masked crime fighters in New York City. In the TV show, he first appeared in 1938, preventing a gang of men from assaulting a couple in an alley in New York. He stopped an armed robbery of a local market just a week later. In 1939, he joined a group of crime fighters named the Minutemen and had an affair with Nelson Gardner, also known as Captain Metropolis. Though he was known as a brutal fighter, Hooded Justice's identity was never known, even after some of his colleagues killed him after a fellow masked fighter framed him for a series of child murders in 1955. Hooded Justice is a towering figure; a large man with broad shoulders, he wore a purple mask over his face with a red hood. However, his distinguishing identifying marker was the noose he had tied around his neck and the rope tied around his waist. Though no one ever knew his identity, many assumed he was of German or German American descent.

This context is important in reference to the beginning of episode 6—in which audiences watch a TV show inside of the *Watchmen* universe, upon which Hooded Justice is interrogated by police detectives about his sexual predilections and unmasks himself as a stereotypical, toned white man. Though he is never unmasked in the original series, this unmasking allows Lindelof to foreshadow the appearance of Hooded Justice in the episode and serves as a metaphor for the racial unmasking of the real Hooded Justice, who exists in the show's universe: a hundred-year-old Black man named Bass Reeves from Tulsa, Oklahoma. By doing this, Lindelof attempts to subvert the racism embedded within comic culture while also rewriting the history of racism in America as one of institutional betrayal.

First, from the comic perspective, Lindelof attempts to rewrite Black identity into the history of the genre. Similar to the racism found within gaming and other popular culture industries, the history of comic books is fraught with white supremacy, anti-Blackness, and lack of diversity. Marc Singer (2002) points out that critics have long proclaimed that comics advance racist stereotypes via repetition (108). Whitney Hunt (2018) finds that major comic book companies, such as Marvel and DC, have received "substantial criticism" over recent years for their unrelenting racist stereotypes (87). Most of the beloved superheroes were born in a more overtly racist era, and while these old comics have their own white supremacist problems, they have not changed much over the years. Arguably, by simply following the same pattern, Marvel and DC let the racist discourse in their older comics reinforce racist attitudes in the twenty-first century. Paradoxically, such a dismal past allows Lindelof the space to recreate the comic, to focus on a more anti-racist—or pro-Blackness—paradigm that moves away from the classically bigoted tropes.

Yet, the framing of Black history as that of institutional betrayal also attempts to reappropriate a vision of white supremacy. The entire ethos of the episode hinges on Bass Reeves seeking justice in an unjust system. Reeves joins the police to enact justice, but the racism of Cyclops (a version of the Ku Klux

Klan in this universe) illustrates to him that the world is unjust. His fellow cops seemingly defend him but are secretly a part of Cyclops. Even after Hooded Justice joins the Minutemen, the first group of masked crime fighters in this universe, he finds out they do not care about either Black trauma or crimes against Black people. To Will Reeves, Bass Reeves's son, the entire world and all of its institutions—especially the ones created to uphold the law—fail to protect Black people. Though most of these encounters are fictional, they still rewrite the history of anti-Black racism, or, perhaps, white supremacy, as a failure of institutions and emphasize intergenerational trauma.

The institutional critique stems from both a police perspective and a superhero perspective. Superhero narratives only exist because the world is unjust (Savov 2014); therefore, having the police be racist in the series is not too far-fetched of a premise and actuality parallels reality. This injustice is what brings Hooded Justice into the crime fighting business—after letting a criminal who is a part of a white nationalist organization go because the police are involved in racist mind control, Reeves is beaten by the same cops who release the white nationalist from handcuffs. The police take Reeves out to a tree and attempt to hang him before cutting him down at the last minute. The cop tells him, "N*****, next time we will not cut you down" (the "n-word" was unbowdlerized in the actual show). While the show posits that Reeves's rage extends from this hate crime, arguably it truly extends from the broader injustice within the police, especially since we know Reeves was the young boy who was obsessed with the black-and-white film in episode 1. After the Tulsa massacre, the lack of police justice, the cruelty of Cyclops, and the lack of faith in his fellow officers, Reeves knows the only way justice can be achieved is if he is the one enacting it. Thus, as he is walking back from nearly being lynched, in shock, the noose still around his neck, he finds a young couple being harassed—and the woman potentially raped—in a back alley. He puts the sheet that the police placed over him back over his head and releases his fury on these three white men, violently overpowering them but not killing them. The rage can be felt, viscerally, in his heavy breathing, and for the first time in his life, justice has been served.

Yet, this narrative also attempts to expand how we view the history of racism as being that of intergenerational trauma. It is not just Bass Reeves who lives through these traumas; his granddaughter, Angela Abar, the protagonist of the story, relives them as well. While episode 6 begins with the interrogation of Hooded Justice in a TV show set in this universe, episode 5 ends with Angela taking her grandfather's "nostalgia," a drug produced to help older people recover their memories. Angela takes all of her grandfather's nostalgia, and outside of the interrogation scene, the rest of episode 6 is dedicated to her "reliving" his life. While this exists as a plot device to reimagine the history of Hooded Justice, it also effectively embodies the abstract nature of intergenerational trauma.

Canadian psychiatrist Vivian Rakoff (1966) found higher than average rates of psychological distress among children of Holocaust survivors. Since then, other researchers have seen similar effects of intergenerational trauma in other contexts. For example, Brent Bezo found that "each generation seemed to kind of learn from the previous one, with survivors telling children, 'Do not trust others, do not trust the world" (qtd. in DeAngelis 2019, 36). For her part, Gilda Graff (2014) writes, "The means of transmission [of intergenerational trauma] has been described in different ways. These include: poor parenting, connected to the master-slave relationship as the template for all human relationships; the dominant one parent family structure created by slavery; and transgenerational haunting . . . Clearly generations of slavery, and of the aftereffects of slavery, including generations of poverty, have all exposed children to toxic stress" (195–96). No matter how you put it, more and more research illustrates the reality of this connective trauma, which Lindelof's Hooded Justice and his granddaughter embody in popular culture.

The show, in fact, presents trauma as the explanation for the cyclical and ever-present nature of racism. As Faulkner once wrote (a quote that is been over-cited, we know, but it still pertinent here): "The past is never dead. It's not even past," and *Watchmen* illustrates this point with astounding accuracy. By having Angela live these memories, the show posits that the trauma her grandfather felt—the explicit racism, the near-lynching, the rage, the betrayal of his police and superhero colleagues, the pain of family lost due to his rage—is hers as well. It composes the fabric of her being. In the present, Angela is dealing with a sinister plot by Cyclops to kill Dr. Manhattan and steal his energy, which parallels the plot in Reeves's past where Cyclops enacts a plot to brainwash Black people into killing each other through using subliminal messages in 8mm films. Angela understands how to react in these situations because she carries her grandfather's trauma with her. It propels her as a justice-seeking, vigilante fighter in the present.

Overall, Lindelof's episodic feature challenges the history of comic book narratives, the *Watchmen* universe, and racism in this country by focusing on Black characters dealing with familial, collective trauma and highlighting the cyclical nature of racism. Scholars and popular authors like Ta-Nehisi Coates (2014), Derrick Bell (1993), and Jessie Daniels (2021) have stated for years that racism is an evolutionary entity—shapeshifting based upon laws, conditions, and values of any given time. Lindelof paints the broader history of the twentieth century with just such a brush, showing that while racism in the 1960s might have been more explicit in nature, it still exists in our contemporary lives. It just might seem more hidden. His series rewrites racism as a phenomenon that invades our histories and popular cultures by sticking to people—not only in their own lives but in their children's and grandchildren's.

Appropriating Symbols and Narratives in Music Videos

While Lindelof's nearly ten-hour series portrays a complex narrative about the history of racism in the United States, counternarratives presented in songs and music videos have performed similar functions (albeit on smaller scales) over the past few years. Two examples come to mind, one better-known than the other: Childish Gambino's "This Is America" and Gary Clark Jr.'s "This Land." Childish Gambino (the stage moniker of the actor/writer/musician Donald Glover) released his rap song and music video in 2018 with critical acclaim from the *Atlantic* (Giorgis 2018), *Rolling Stone* (Johnson 2018), and NPR's *All Things Considered* (Carmichael 2018), among others. The simple lyrics of the song are meant to display the realities of violence in Black America, while the music video juxtaposes these harsh truths by combining engrossing, lively dancing with depictions of racism and brutality in the background. Whereas Gambino creates counternarratives of race in America via abstraction, Gary Clark Jr. focuses more on tangible metaphors in his rock song "This Land," released in 2019. The song's lyrics focus on Clark's experiences living in conservative Texas during the Trump era; meanwhile, the music video appropriates images of the Confederacy and lynching history (such as Confederate flags and nooses) to counter white interpretations of who "owns" the USA. Together, both these songs reappropriate tropes of white supremacy in order to claim agency in their own histories and stories—giving a proverbial (or in Clark's case a literal) "fuck you" to people who either act like racism is no problem or claim that it is just something that was true in the past.

In the beginning of Gambino's music video (fig. 17), a Black guitarist sits in a chair in an empty warehouse and strums a cheerful, playful beat. In the background, a choir creates a lighthearted melody by repeating "yeah, yeah, yeah" in different tones. Gambino then appears and dances—seemingly awkwardly—toward the man, until he eventually pulls out a pistol and shoots the guitarist, who is now wearing a mask and a noose around his neck, in the head. This is where the tone of the song and the video change drastically to a trap rap style. The lyrics focus on wanting to get money, dancing, and singing, and ultimately having a good time. Yet this first minute of the four-minute video is supposed to be interpreted as an enticement, a way of setting up the main theme: that white people do not care about Black deaths. In this interpretation, Childish Gambino embodies the dichotomy between his own Black experiences and the white gaze, moving seamlessly from Black cultural scene to Black cultural scene, participating in the murder of multiple Black folks, in order to show how white supremacy numbs white people into dehumanizing Black experiences and Black death (Garneni 2020). In short, this opening scene allows Gambino to embody white apathy toward the Black people in general terms. When he shoots and kills the guitarist as the introduction to the trap and raps the titular phrase, "this is America," he's not pointing to the idea of killing someone as uniquely American, but rather to the idea of white people not caring about Black deaths as uniquely American.

Figure 17. Still shot from Childish Gambino's "This Is America" music video. Childish Gambino stands in front of a church choir before shooting all of its members with an assault rifle.

This is further evidenced at the 1:40 mark, when a Black church choir sings "go tell somebody" to "get your money, Black man." The choir grooves on a small stage in front of a wall and door in the same warehouse as the rest of the video. Gambino emerges from the door and looks at the choir, as if wondering if he is in the right space. He then swerves to the music as he makes his way in front of the choir as they repeat the phrase "get your money, Black man." His smile and pleasant demeanor fade at the 1:55 mark, and someone throws him an assault rifle that he uses to massacre the choir behind him. His repeated line into the second verse—"this is America"—feels despondent now, as if it is just something that he is telling himself. Up to this point, audiences might not know how to interpret Gambino's persona in the video; yet this scene paints a picture that only comes from white rage. There are no historical or contemporary examples of Black-on-Black massacres. However, there was a then-recent example of a young white man, Dylann Roof, entering the Emanuel AME Church in Charleston, South Carolina, and killing nine Black people at a Bible study class. The parallels between that massacre and some of what is depicted in the video, only three years removed from the shooting, were obvious to many people online (Koyer 2019). In this context then, we cannot interpret Gambino as solely being a Black actor in the video. He encompasses some aspects of whiteness as well. In this sense, we can understand the murder of the choir not only as the daily violence characteristic of our society but also as an example of how we do not care about these deaths to make change. The victims die and are forgotten and people move on. Apathy is the central controlling theme.

All of this is to say that in Gambino's music video, he appropriates what white people think about Black people—they are "thugs," murderers, criminals, and people who do not care about the "violence" in their own communities—and flips it as a critique of whiteness and white supremacy itself. His movements throughout the video can thus be interpreted in the ways white people depict Black people in popular culture and everyday life. The phrase "this is America" does not mean that this is literally the United States; rather, this is what white people think about Black people in this country. Gambino attempts to hold up a mirror to the white gaze trained on his race to pinpoint the racism embedded within white sight. From a countermemory perspective, Gambino appropriates historical narratives and tropes to challenge how white audiences engage with art and history. The point is to challenge them.

However, this appropriation from a figurative perspective comes with a big risk, since many have to look underneath the surface to fully understand Gambino's message. It is doubtful that many people saw this framework; it is possible that they instead interpreted the hyperviolence as Gambino's critique of Blackness or maybe as nothing at all. Nevertheless, the way Gambino uses violence in his song and music video demonstrates how the appropriation of white gazes can create thoughtful art.

Clark's song and music video appropriates white history and tropes more explicitly. The video begins with an electric guitar being strummed in the background as a Black child rides in the backseat of a car and watches scenes around rural America—the American flag and Texas flag, church signs, and small Confederate flags on a mailbox. The camera lingers on the child's face as he witnesses the Confederate flags, asking audiences to ponder what such a flag would mean to a young Black child. The interlude leads to the actual song, where the Black boy baptizes himself and wakes up in a field. In the first verse, Clark sings about living in "Trump country" and how white people "cannot wait to call the police on me." He creates a vision of how tough it is to live in these spaces as a Black person. Yet, most importantly, he also appropriates lynching memory in the video section that corresponds with this first verse. At the 1:30 mark, the Black boy, now sweaty from running through a field, looks up at a massive oak tree and sees a rope tied around one of the branches—a clear connection to lynching vestiges of the past. Obviously, such a rope would conjure fear and pain in anyone who understands the history. However, the next scene shows a different Black boy swinging on the rope as two children sit in the tree above him, turning the rope and tree into an act of innocence and child's play. This video section corresponds with Clark telling a white audience, "this is mine now, legit / I ain't leaving here, you cannot take it from me." He demonstrates his own agency in telling white supremacy to "fuck off" and does so by taking the symbol of the rope and claiming it as his own. The nooses do not hold the same symbolic meaning if you employ them as a toy.

The chorus of the song reads: "N***** run, N****** run / Go back where you come from / We do not want, we do not want your kind / We think you's a dog born / Fuck you, I am America's son / This is where I come from," and ends with Clark repeating "this land is mine" (the "n-word" was unbowdlerized in the actual song). The chorus allows Clark to follow an appropriating form—especially when it comes to claiming who is "America's son" and stating, "this land is mine." Of course, claiming to be "America's son" is an attempt to recapture what it means to be American. Most white nationalist rhetoric revolves around claiming the United States as a white country (Serwer 2019; Bouie 2017). Therefore, in calling himself "America's son" Clark seeks to enrage white people who believe this country is uniquely theirs. (Of course, the "fuck you" before this line performs the same function). And in calling this land "mine," Clark takes a step forward in claiming space in this country.

Overall, Clark's approach takes the emblems of the Confederacy and the Jim Crow era (lynching and Confederate symbols) and openly ridicules them as white supremacist tools. Not too long ago, he would never have had the opportunity to have such a mass audience through music or a music video; he would never have been able to take such a public stance against people who literally want to kill him or see him out of the United States. His video thus shows what can change with time—allowing him to take these images of hate and reappropriate them as symbols of empowerment.

Recentering Lynching History in Ken Gonzales-Day's Artwork

While these digital texts reappropriate white supremacist iconography to create compelling and challenging narratives or overt political statements, other types of media can perform similar functions, even with less discursive text. I (James) remember the moment I first came across a specific art series that has been a tangent in my research for the past five years or so. I was working on a conference presentation dealing with the erasure of Latinx lynchings in the American imaginary, and as someone who is dedicated to tying visceral affect with discursive argument, I was looking at images on Google that could potentially benefit my talk. As I did so, I came across an image that stuck with me because something was effectively missing (fig. 18).

Figure 18. *Disguised Bandit* (2006) is part of Ken Gonzales-Day's *Erased Lynching* series, in which the artist digitally erased images of lynched bodies to speak to America's lynching history.

I was struck by the absence in the photograph. The descriptor "Disguised Bandit" clearly suggests that the original photograph contained a lynched individual ("bandit" invoking a Latinx individual, especially in such a desolate landscape), and the posture of those in the image parallels other lynching photographs I had seen in the past. Without knowing the context of Ken Gonzales-Day or his series, I still felt compelled by this image. Not only did I sense the speculative nature of the white faces—that the white men felt so proud or happy that they wanted to pose in a lynching photograph—but also it connected to my feelings about the erasure of Latinx lynchings, that most people might just assume the removed body would be Black. I quickly became a believer and advocate of Gonzales-Day's work.

In his series, Gonzales-Day "upends expectations about the geography and targets of lynching." As Berger (2012) points out, "its location is the American West, not the Deep South, and its victims are Mexican, not African-American." Gonzales-Day writes on his website, "The series is notable for its use of historic images, in which I have used digital technology (Photoshop) to erase the lynching victim and rope from historic depictions of lynchings, from etchings, historic photographs, and postcards, collected over the past twenty years. By erasing the victim's bodies, I sought to create a visual experience that would force the viewer to focus on the crowd and in doing so, to address the underlying racism and bias that was foundational to these acts of collective violence, which have increasingly come to be seen as central to understanding of race and difference in America." The artwork was created to raise awareness and to help viewers visualize whiteness by drawing attention to what is missing, absent, erased. Rather than revictimizing those murdered in such collective and often premeditated acts of killing, the work allows the viewer to literally focus on the crowd—complete with jeering and smiling faces, and hopes to promote a critical exploration of American history (Gonzales-Day 2021). According to Gonzales-Day, the erasure of racialized bodies, specifically Latinx bodies, could help recenter a narrative that is not often discussed in American history while emphasizing why white audiences enjoy consuming imagery of racialized deaths.

While Gonzales-Day does not explicitly discuss how he appropriates these images for art with a political message, his work challenges the history of lynching by presenting it as more complex than just white versus Black history, refocusing it rather on the sins of whiteness. First, the Black and white binary exists for many different reasons, but rhetorically, it benefits white people because it implies that racism is only against one set of people (Sanchez 2025). Juan Perea (1997) defines the binary as "the conception that race in America consists, either exclusively or primarily, of only two constituent racial groups, the Black and White . . . In addition, the paradigm dictates that all other racial groups in the United States are best understood through the Black/White binary paradigm" (361). Perea illustrates the problem as a lack of understanding of race in the United States, but Gonzales-Day's art series further demonstrates how the binary benefits white understandings of history. If someone saw these photos in their proper context, they would be faced with the realization that Latinx lynchings occurred at high rates in this country too, and that the historical narratives the viewers learned in high school history were wrong. Erasing the Brown body from the photographs thus symbolizes effectively what America has done with this history, turning lynching solely into a Black-and- white issue. Gonzales-Day's removal of Latinx victims from the photos thus attempts to illustrate the lack of understanding of lynching history.

His art also refocuses on the ways whiteness makes a spectacle of lynching. Most Americans know at least bits and pieces of Jim Crow and lynching history, but do not center so much on the spectacle. Lynching was often about demonstrating power, which can be seen in not only people wanting to take photos during these events (illustrating their power permanently) but in making many of these photos into postcards. Ersula Ore (2019) writes, "By facilitating the circulation of lynching postcards, the federal government demonstrated its adherence to the politics that sustained white supremacy" (64). The entire purpose of a postcard, rhetorically speaking, is to engage with another individual, often by sharing a photo of a popular place, a beautiful scene, or shared ideology. Under a spectacle lens of lynching history, then, the fact that lynching postcards were so readily available in the early parts of the twentieth century suggests that the practice of lynching itself was not about a warped sense of justice or mob rule; it was about the display of violence, or "circulatory violence" as Mark Simpson (2004) would define it.

Therefore, Gonzales-Day appropriates these images of racist histories to illustrate what we forget about lynching history: different racialized victims, the spectacle, and the circulation of violent images. The act itself challenges misconceptions and preconceived notions of lynching histories, reframing it around mobs of white violence. While Childish Gambino's music video highlights what white audiences currently think of Black-on-Black violence (and its oversensationalization), Gonzales-Day's work emphasizes what white audiences wish to forget about their own extremely violent histories. In some sense, by erasing the victim, he forces audiences to engage and remember. Rhetorically, this positions audiences to forgo the typical ontologies of art criticism—where judgment feels entirely personal and subjective—to, instead, view the art as the beholder of a larger truth of the past.

Counterappropriation as Provocative Method

Our analysis has led us to conclude that for artists of any kind—musicians, digital artists, filmmakers, and more—counterappropriation exists as a method to propel anti-racist and countermemory narratives. All the artists discussed earlier in the chapter aim to be provocative in one way or another. Whether it be stepping on Confederate flags in a music video or telling a fictional version of racist history in the United States or erasing the deaths of Black and Brown bodies in lynching photographs to highlight the spectacle of the white gaze, these artists use provocation as a method of not only engaging with audiences but also retelling American history via appropriation. It is important to note that, of course, we are not arguing that we understand some perceived intent on the part of each of these artists that has never been publicly stated before. Rather, our analysis stems from the perceived provocation that is central to the narrative each artist presents. *Watchmen*'s central narrative could have existed without the Hooded Justice episode, which is a stand-alone story, but, obviously, Lindelof found this storyline important enough (and probably controversial enough) to make it one of nine episodes in a limited series. Brian Hiatt (2019) writes that "Damon Lindelof's decision to play racial injustice (and the politics of masks) at the core of HBO's *Watchmen* starts to seem deeply rooted in the text. It also makes episode Six's audacious retcon of Hooded Justice all the more intriguing."

By unmasking Hooded Justice and delivering a history of American racism in this episode, Lindelof invites audiences to explore this history for themselves. Childish Gambino and Gary Clark Jr. do not necessarily need music videos to accompany their singles, yet the counterappropriations they use in their music videos is what made their music culturally relevant and highly discussed on social media and in think pieces (Rao 2018; St. Felix 2018; Martin, DeSoto, and Morris 2019). For instance, Sarah Lindmark (2019) states, "Gambino's music video plays with his audience's understanding of musical genre, crime, and mass media by visually placing these concepts in the video's foreground without including the concrete referential material the audience might expect from a hip hop music video. In doing so, he shows his audience that senseless gun violence, the distractions of social media, and the vacuity of popular music have become normalized aspects of our everyday lives" (28–29). In this sense, Gambino "playing" with expectations is what leads people to think through the countermemories he presents. Lastly, and on the other hand, Gonzales-Day's exhibit would not exist outside of the provocation; the tension of the erasure is pivotal to the exhibit's structure.

Each of these popular culture artifacts thus utilizes provocation as a countermemory method. More specifically, we contend that the artists involved perform counterappropriation as means to get audiences more engaged with lesser known racial histories and memories, talking about the Tulsa Black Massacre, the lynchings of Latinx and Black people, the exploitation of Black murder in the media, and Confederate memorabilia discourse. While none of the artistic expressions examined exist solely to be educational or informational, their counterappropriations inherently perform that function using forgotten histories, memories, or moments to add intrigue into their narratives. This leads many audiences to ask, "Wait, did this really happen?" What actually happened in Tulsa? What is the history of racial passing—and hiding—in this country? How many Latinx people were lynched in the Southwest? How has the Confederate flag been used as a tool of oppression? How does the media frame massacre and Black/hip hop culture? While there might be some viewers who do not come to these questions, the various think-pieces and press garnered by these various artforms illustrate the extent to which they influenced the zeitgeist.

As a method, counterappropriation disrupts how audiences engage with countermemory. Counterappropriation is not as concrete in the countermemory claims as public memorials, countermaps, and other objects and sites discussed in this book. The countermemory is often secondary and interpretative. Audiences need to seek more information in order to completely engage with it. Yet, what makes counterappropriation unique is that way it engages with audiences who come to these narratives and exhibits without a specific interest in countermemory. No one watches *Watchmen* or Childish Gambino's or Gary Clark Jr.'s music videos for the discourse on memory. They are brought in because of the provocation, the interesting storytelling, or the hype, and then engage with the memories. Gonzales-Day's art exhibit is a bit different than these other pieces because some audiences *might* seek engagement with the art for its argument about memory, but they are more likely to come to it for its visceral performance than anything else. As Maurice Berger (2012) noted about Gonzales-Day's exhibit, it "reminds us, too, of the power of time to erase history, in part because it is our instinct to forget the events that expose our intolerance, indifference or depravity. But it also urges us to put our own history into a story that few of us know. More than anything, it makes us think where our ancestors—or own bodies—might belong: as a victim dangling above or a perpetrator grinning below." Overall, as a method, counterappropriation changes how audiences engage and research memories.

Audiences that engage with these texts thus become agents who learn and teach others about histories that are often not taught in schools via texts that are more palatable than academic books and articles. The virality of the counterappropriations means that audiences do not have to visit physical sites and spaces in order to engage; they just have to click a few buttons on their phones, computers, or TVs. This makes these texts inherently more accessible for an average viewer, too. Thus, counterappropriation can be viewed as a closely aligned rhetorical force of countermemory—often with similar goals and causes for engagement—but without the explicit intentions and symbolism. As a method, it works more in the background of popular culture artifacts, not often as the main driving force, but as the lesson learned via these unique engagements and narratives.

Conclusion

When people generally think of countermemory, they often picture statues, museums, or perhaps public spaces. These are the sites most analyses on countermemory have explored over the past decades. However, most people generally do not think about how consuming popular culture, especially TV shows or music, might try to shape views of memory. We can assume that most people did not take to Gambino's or Clark's songs or Lindelof's series seeking countermemory. They were interested in the comic culture or Lindelof's previous TV series, or perhaps they were already devotees of these artists or wanted to capitalize on the chatter surrounding them. Yet, as the pieces discussed in this chapter garnered traction, they attracted larger audiences, people who were interested in the history of Tulsa, or the juxtaposition of racialized violence in "This Is America," or the mockery of the Confederacy in "This Land." People probably did not initially seek these artifacts to learn, but after the first wave of press came through, later audiences did exactly just that.

However, more importantly, these popular culture artifacts live as edifices to countermemory, as a way to extend plot or video narrative or art's meaning. Countermemory, therefore, is not always about memory or historical narratives themselves. It can be about the appropriation of cultural artifacts that represent something historical. What makes these appropriations interesting is how they attempt to unite a message about history with a larger point. Lindelof points to the generational trauma of racism; Gambino acknowledges our culture's lack of care about it; Clark claims his own space in a country that does not claim him; and Gonzales-Day displays the erasure of Latinx lynching history. All four appropriate various forms—historical narratives, symbols, photographs, and recent tragedies—to show us a side of history we have not seen before or pull us into new feelings and thoughts on our current state. Where most other uses of countermemory are attempting to explicitly rewrite a narrative, in popular culture, to the artist here seek to incite a visceral response or connect the audience to a specific feeling. The interest in the actual memories and histories is secondary.

To close, in Lindelof's series *The Leftovers*, a series in which 2 percent of the world has vanished in the blink of an eye, a new religion/cult forms, called the Guilty Remnant. This group exists ambiguously in the world, never speaking out loud, only communicating through pen and paper, and smoking "to proclaim our faith," though we are never sure what that faith is. They are agitators, acting on the people trying to get back to their lives five years after the vanishing. They consistently disrupt everyone else's norms, customs, and healing because they define their existence as "living reminders." It takes a while for an audience to understand the symbolism, but at the heart of the Guilty Remnant is an understanding that the vanishing utterly destroyed humanity and civilization. Furthermore, *The Leftovers* illustrates that by not embracing the absurdity of the lives, the remnant are currently living in a mode that is more absurd than trying to move forward. They "live" to "remind" people of what happened and that nothing they can do will ever allow them to collectively forget it.

We do not want to concretely connect the popular culture artifacts we studied in this chapter with *The Leftovers*, but these artifacts are living reminders too. They "live" in the realm of media—appealing to people to write stories about them, to further connect with their narratives, to discuss them with their friends and families. They are active in influencing people. Yet they also remind us of the histories we forget and erase, the narratives that fall to the wayside due to oppressive remembering or active forgetting. They remind us that history is never fully known, and that we can use their art to further explore parts of the past.

They are living reminders of how often major historical moments and symbols are taken for granted and urge people to engage with them, in any capacity or mode.

4

Absences and Presences

A Countermemory Tour of East Texas

The tourism industry in the United States is built around consumption: consumption of culture, foods, and narratives. I (James) distinctly remember being a tourist in Washington, DC, during my first year of grad school, while speaking at a conference. With so many museums, memorials, and public exhibits to see, I was not sure which to visit with only one full day dedicated to tourism in the city. I settled on the Lincoln Memorial and National Mall, two spots enshrined in my understanding of American history. Visiting these spaces, I recalled what it was to be "American"—reflecting on memories of Martin Luther King delivering his "I Have a Dream" speech, thinking about the "forefathers" of American history, and buying into the American exceptionalism narrative. I consumed what the designers of these spaces rhetorically constructed for me to consume, but also, still, a variation of it—one in which King co-opted the National Mall for his own vision of American progress. The purpose of these DC tourism sites is for audiences to absorb the displayed history, to effectively buy into a shared understanding of the past and of each other. As Tim Gruenewald (2021) identifies, though, even as tourists visit the National Mall and observe many buildings that were erected from the labor of enslaved individuals, there is still no historical marker on the Mall indicating this vital knowledge (204).

As we know, the tourism industry is built around lies, half-truths, and grandiose myths. The narratives white Americans tell the rest of America about whose legacies are worthy of remembrance, which stories are significant enough to merit towering monuments in parks and town squares, and which lives matter in the public record are found in every major city and community. It is particularly evident in the American South and Texas. The result is a city like Savannah, Georgia—arguably one of the most aesthetically pleasing southern cities, which boasts twenty-two public town squares across one square mile in the downtown area. Each mini-park is dedicated to one white man after another: James Edward Oglethorpe, Casimir Pulaski, Jefferson Davis, and on and on. While there are increasing numbers of markers devoted to Black history in Savannah (especially after Abigail Jordan's advocacy led to the African American monument finally being constructed in 2002), there is little open, honest discussion about Savannah's role in the slave trade or the glaring fact that the opulent wealth on display with the countless mansions is a direct result of slavery. The overt socioeconomic disparities that exist in the city still—disparities that overwhelmingly fall on racialized lines—and the lack of discussion of who gets celebrated in the city both indicate nothing seems to be changing.

While in Savannah recently, I (April) sought out the Weeping Time historical marker, which was dedicated in 2007. The title "Weeping Time" remembers March 2 and 3, 1859, the dates of the largest recorded slave auction in the United States with over four hundred men, women, and children sold into slavery. The marker is located several miles outside the historic district in a predominantly Black neighborhood. I recognize that the Georgia Historical Society researched the location where this event occurred and acknowledge the importance of placing the marker as close as possible to the actual location, but I cannot help but think that the location is convenient for the tourism industry in Savannah. No tourists are going to stumble across this marker while on a Savannah tour and thus learn about this event, and there are certainly no markers, monuments, or memorials in the city limits that discuss the horrors of slavery other than the African American monument (and it took Jordan eleven years of fighting with the city to get that artifact placed by the Savannah River in a bustling, touristy area). The Weeping Time marker, while a significant accomplishment for activists in Savannah, cannot compete with the other twenty-two squares in the historic district that utterly erase slavery, racial terror lynching, and Jim Crow from public memory. What we have described in Savannah is also echoed across the southern United States, so it is not an aberrant tourism situation unique to one city. And while sites of countermemory are slowly emerging around the region—from the NMPJ in Alabama to Whitney Plantation in Louisiana to the Owens-Thomas House and Slave Quarters tour in Georgia—there are still many histories and memories dedicated to people of color that must enter the public sphere.

Thus, for this final chapter, we present a countermemory tour of East Texas, looking at five specific sites that have varying connections with countermemories. While some of these narratives have been communicated to the public, most are either erased or minimized from public memory. As a digital accompaniment and interactive feature to this chapter, we have composed a countermemory tour using ArcGIS (fig.19). The purpose of this countertour is twofold: 1) to show what comes from building countermemory tourways—the ways we

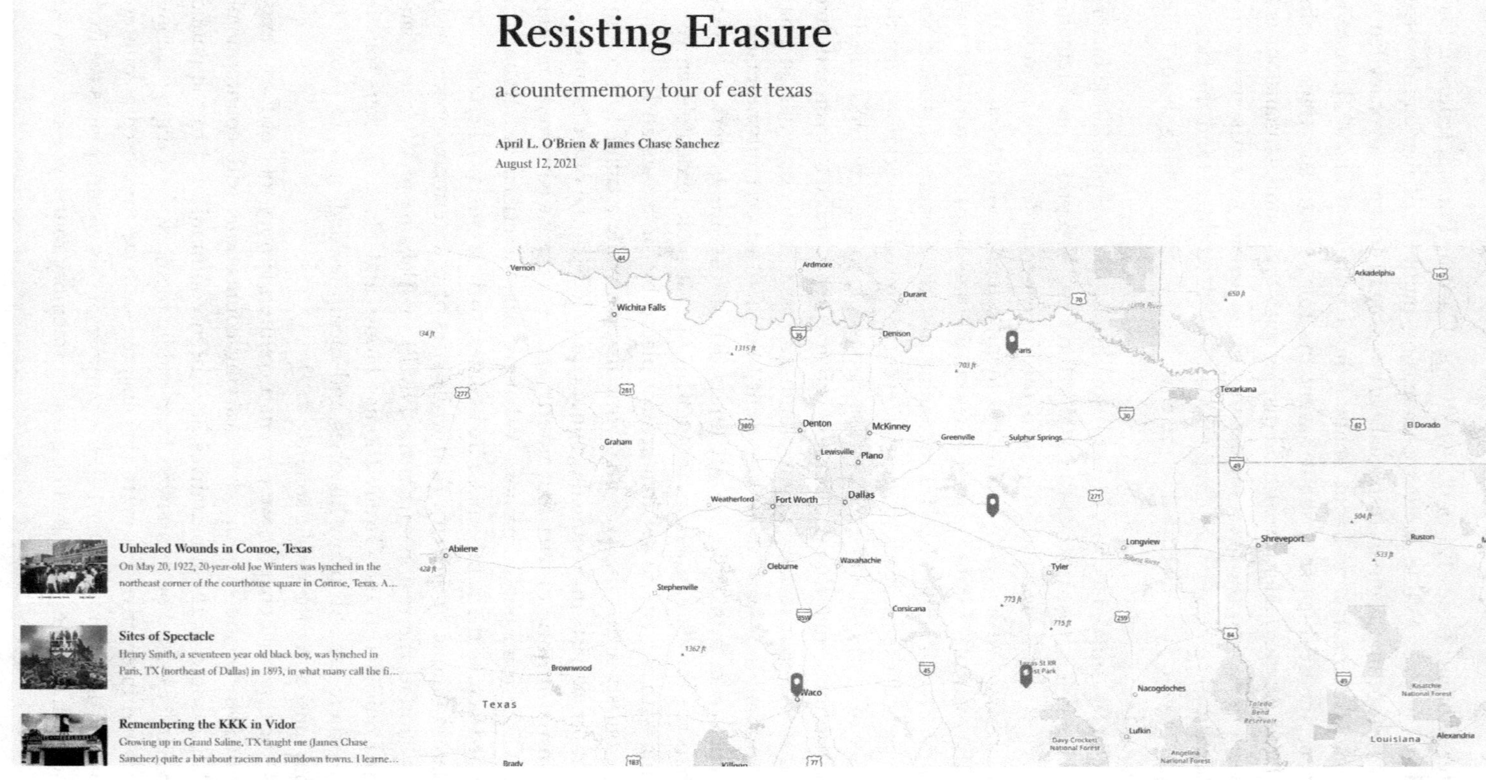

Figure 19. Screenshot of countermemory tour; created by April O'Brien and James Chase Sanchez.

can reimagine spaces and communities through interconnected countermemories that each community erases or forgets; and 2) to illustrate what tourists can learn by locating what is present and absent on the trip. We create this countertour for people to engage with via this book or in person, if possible, and to see what does—and does not—exist in these places. Countermemory tours are as much about what is not seen as they are about what is seen. *The absences create meaning as much as the presences do*. People can better understand a community's values by what they commemorate—or choose to forget or erase—publicly. More specifically, we contend that such tours are inherently community-driven and community dependent. This chapter exists as a call for people to look in their own communities to see what stories and histories are managed, mismanaged, or erased.

These sites and cities span across hundreds of miles in the Piney Woods of East Texas. While there is no singular order to visiting these spaces, we have decided to go from north to south, generally, with the first site being in the most northern part of East Texas and the final being in the most southern.

On Spectacles and Erasures in Paris

Our tour begins in Paris, Texas, northeast of Dallas. Henry Smith, a seventeen-year-old Black boy, was lynched in Paris in 1893, in what many call the first spectacle lynching in the United States. Smith was accused of raping and killing a young white girl, Myrtle, the daughter of a local deputy, Henry Vance. A manhunt quickly ensued to find Smith, who allegedly had a run-in with Henry a few months prior and supposedly swore to take vengeance against the deputy (which could never be proven). Smith left town when he heard authorities were on the hunt for him and was caught a few days later in rural Arkansas, at which time he allegedly confessed to the crime on a train back to Paris. As of today, no evidence links Smith to the crime.

Upon his return to Paris, Smith was tortured by a white lynch mob. They took him to the fairgrounds, right outside of the town center, where they created a lynching scaffold with "Justice" painted on it. The white men mutilated his body in various ways we will not describe here and cheered upon his whimpers. Eventually, the mob poured oil on him and the scaffold and lit a fire, waiting until Smith burned to death before extinguishing it. Best estimates suggest that anywhere from ten thousand to fifteen thousand people took part in the lynch mob, with many coming from Dallas and other nearby cities to participate. Reporters from northern newspapers covered the event, making it a national story, with many in the north referring to the lynching as a national disgrace.

When I (James) stand now near the spot where Smith was burned alive in the old fairgrounds, I feel . . . empty. Paris uses the same space for the fairgrounds as the town did 130 years ago. Though the buildings near the bare field have changed over the years, the field itself has not: a flat, open pasture with a few dead trees spread out a hundred feet from one another. The history of Henry's death cannot be felt in this space because there is no marker or historical context describing what happened. No acknowledgement of this historical misdeed lingers nearby. Most who traverse these grounds during the annual fair in the fall and during other local events probably have never heard of either Smith or the history haunting this space and place. It has been consciously erased, scrubbed over by the state and the local community.

What marks Smith's lynching as the one of the nadirs of race relations in the United States is not that so many people called for his death—racist mob rule occurred quite often at the turn of the twentieth century. Rather, the *spectacle* of the event, the thousands of people who descended to his lynching to watch Smith be tortured and murdered, illustrates the hard truth that lynching was not an abomination to these people; they actively enjoyed it and took pleasure in viewing it. How do we remember this spectacle lynching in the United States when there is not even a marker or historical context tied to the site? How do we remember this tragedy, which many dubbed a "holocaust" at the time (Bills 2015), when Paris is so quick to forget? What is a spectacle if it is forgotten?

By definition, a spectacle attracts people to a particular site, be it an event, a performance, or something else. Though Texas governor Jim Hogg publicly denounced the lynching at the time and told local police to arrest and charge the people who propagated it, the residents of Paris and surrounding areas were undoubtedly proud of Henry's murder. It is the best-known historical fact about Paris, one that citizens would not want to be front and center in their twenty-first-century reality (no one wants the worst of their history displayed), but there is a certain irony that residents were so proud of a murder a century ago that drew thousands of people from miles away (without cars, mind you), whereas in the present, the descendants are either too ashamed of or too removed from the event to discuss it.

Paris should not be enshrined as the capital of spectacle lynchings in the United States, and, if precedence holds with Grand Saline and Slocum (regarding the attitudes of white residents), this is what many white residents would claim about a public marker denoting the tragedy that occurred on the local fairgrounds. But history and public memory are not always easy. Remembering our collective wrongs is just as important as remembering when we were right. It is easy for citizens of Paris and passersby to weave through their daily lives without much confrontation with the past, but if we can make a spectacle out of murder, we should make a spectacle out of remembrance too. Since no public memory enshrines Smith's death, audiences must assume Paris does not care about the tragedy that unfolded in the community over a century ago. Citizens now participate in a collective amnesia, celebrating, in a sense, a collective memory by erasing it from any public view at all. The values of Paris are located in that empty fairgrounds lot, where anyone wanting to learn about Smith will walk away empty-handed. For the gatekeepers of this community, silence is the answer to injustice. The silence, then, is our countermemory.

TikTok Activism and Remembering Jesse Washington in Waco

While researching the Texas Historical Commission for an article, I (April) performed a content and discourse analysis of the historical marker texts (HMT) in Texas. As part of that analysis, I chose a variety of keywords related to countermemory. One of those terms was lynch(ing), because I wanted to uncover how many HMTs communicate information about these events, the impact and significance of BIPOC individuals, and racialized injustices in Texan history. Upon searching the THC's Atlas database, I found only two HMTs that used the word lynch, and in both cases, the events did not describe racial terror lynching but rather the lynching of white men accused of criminal activity. However, during this research, I discovered that the THC approved an HMT to memorialize Jesse Washington in Waco, Texas—in 2016. As of the summer of 2020, the HMT was supposed to be erected in the coming months. During 2021, the HMT was not installed, which caused a stir among the Community Race Relations Committee in Waco, as well as on social media. For example, TikTok star Colin Browen used his platform to lobby for an HMT to be placed in Waco to recall the lynching of Jesse Washington. In a TikTok video Browen stated the following: "Jesse Washington was tried by an all-white jury and found guilty of murder in four minutes. He was then dragged out of the Waco, Texas, courthouse he was found guilty in by a chain. While he was being dragged, people were hitting him with shovels and stabbing him and he was brought to this tree. In 2016 the Texas Historical Commission announced that they were going to erect a marker commemorating Jesse Washington's death but it was never built. To move forward in society, we have to acknowledge the dark history, learn from it and then strive as hard as we can to not repeat it." Browen's description of Washington's lynching and his call for action were timely, but there is no way to adequately communicate the horror of Washington's murder with words. After years of delays, the marker was finally dedicated in February 2023 (Saegert 2023).

The images (available online via the website Lynching in Texas) from national newspapers are horrific and depict a violent murder in Waco that was attended by fifteen thousand men, women, and children. One photo, captured by the *Waco Times Herald*, depicts Washington's charred and mutilated body in the foreground with a crowd of white men in the background, dressed in suits, ties, and dress hats. Two figures in particular stand out on the right side of the photo—a young white man (possibly fourteen or fifteen years old) smirking at the body and an older white man nearby, wearing a similar grin. The juxtaposition of these images is jarring. But even more disturbing is that for decades the city of Waco made no movement toward acknowledging this historical event and the complicity of many individuals as part of this crime, and their postponement of the marker dedication further polarized activists who wanted this memoryscape amended.

The fact that Washington's murder (and over twenty others in the Waco area alone) was not publicly acknowledged for over one hundred years illustrates a coldness, a cruelty that cannot be overlooked. Since public memory cannot be hermetically sealed either from historical events or from current attitudes, we must consider the voter suppression and anti-CRT laws that Texas legislators attempted to pass during 2021—laws that directly impact the lived experiences of Black Texans and other multiply marginalized individuals. Likewise, Texas SB 17 was passed in 2023 to ban diversity, equity, and inclusion offices in public universities. And while these legislators are fighting to limit opportunities for voting and to promote less transparency, making it difficult to even discuss events like Jesse Washington's lynching, nothing is done to remember the senseless murder of a seventeen-year-old boy in 1916. It may seem counterintuitive that a historical marker dedicated to Jesse Washington could be empowering to the Black community in Waco. However, the act of openly and honestly creating spaces for honest dialogue about actual historical events goes a long way toward promoting healing in cities like Waco. As the EJI reiterates daily in their social media posts, "To overcome racial inequality, we must confront our history." There is no way forward without a reckoning with the past. But how can we inspire a reckoning with injustices when our government is actively seeking ways to prevent us from discussing these matters? In the face of historical commissions that circumvent (or slow down to the point of almost no movement at all) any attempts to produce historical markers that communicate events like Jesse Washington's murder to large-scale attacks on critical theory, it can feel like a losing battle.

But Jesse Washington—and the other hundreds of human beings who were lynched in Texas between 1877 and 1950—deserve more from us. If it takes TikTok activism, coalitions from within communities, and the work of the EJI to get these markers placed, then it is what must be done. On the other hand, though, we cannot ignore the length of time it took the city to decide to place the marker or the fact that it took the efforts of social media activists and community coalitions to place and dedicate the marker. The city's obvious reluctance to take part in truth-telling efforts is underscored by the impact of community workers who were persistent in their fight to remember the legacies of Jesse Washington and so many others.

Local Fights to Remember in Conroe

On May 20, 1922, twenty-year-old Joe Winters, a Black man, was lynched in the northeast corner of the courthouse square in Conroe, Texas. A local newspaper noted that a crowd "larger than the annual visit of the circus" attended the lynching; many of the men wore dress clothes, including hats, dress shirts, and ties. Thousands of white residents attended, among them many women and children. As in most mob-incited acts of racial terror, merely the accusation of an offense was enough to condemn Winters to a brutal death. Accused of attacking a fourteen-year-old white girl, Winters received no trial and was burned to death in the public square (Lynching in Texas Staff n.d.). Winters's death also comprised one of eight lynchings that occurred in Texas in the second half of May 1922 alone, which illustrates the rampant violence commonplace in Texas and the South during the first half of the twentieth century ("Two Negroes Lynched" 1922).

The *Chicago Defender*, a Black-owned newspaper, depicted a much different narrative than that of the whitestream media, though. John Jones, a writer for the *Defender*, describes how the record-breaking number of lynchings in a two-week period in May 1922 put "the entire populace on edge." Throughout the region, the Black community viewed these acts of violence as a sign that the KKK's influence was "flowering" and being allowed to grow in power and number in East Texas. Jones also notes the "ease with which the innocent captives and suspects were forced from the sheriff" illustrated that "the law has given up" on dealing with mob violence. The article depicts the beginning of the Great Migration, as many Black Texans began to leave the plantations where they had labored and head for northern states. Jones describes a man named John Turner, who could "stand it no longer" after seeing three men burned near Corsicana, Texas. Gathering up his wife and two children, he set out for St. Paul, Minnesota, to live with a cousin. Jones also recounts the inherent danger that Black Texans encountered as they attempted to leave the region; they feared that if the whites learned of their plans, they would increase their violent persecution.

Nearly one hundred years later, Conroe still bears the wounds of Joe Winters's lynching. While the city may appear to be more diverse (with close to 28 percent Hispanic residents and 12 percent Black residents), like most spaces in the United States, it is obviously segregated. The University of Virginia's Racial Dot map (currently not online due to new information from the 2020 census) illustrated that Hispanic and Black residents live on the east side of Conroe and white residents live on the west side, closer to Lake Conroe. The Winters case was also not an isolated incident of racialized violence here; Conroe is a town plagued with racist historical events. In 1981, a maintenance worker at Conroe High School, Clarence Brandley, was wrongfully convicted of the rape and murder of a white high school student, sixteen-year-old Cheryl Fergeson. Like many such cases in US history, the case, "driven by racial prejudice, bad lawyering and shoddy evidence," centered around racism and white female purity (Blakinger 2018). As he was the only Black janitor (out of five) among the suspects, the authorities focused their attention almost entirely on Brandley. According to Blakinger, a Texas Ranger reportedly said these words to Brandley: "Since you're the n****, you're elected" (the "n-word" was bowdlerized as shown in Blakinger's article). In 1987, State District Judge Perry Pickett wrote, "No case has presented a more shocking scenario of the effects of racial prejudice, perjured testimony, witness intimidation (and) an investigation the outcome of which was predetermined" (qtd. in Blakinger 2018). Likewise, the Texas Court of Criminal Appeals stated that Brandley's trial lacked "the rudiments of fairness." Thanks to the efforts of New Jersey-based Centurion Ministries, the case was ultimately thrown out, and Brandley was released from prison (where he was on death row) in 1990. However, Brandley was never granted a pardon or received any financial compensation the ten years he served in prison (Hall 2018).

Both Joe Winters's lynching and Clarence Brandley's near-lynching have been scratched from the public memory. As of 2023, District Attorney James Keeshan still practices law in Conroe, in spite of the unethical practice of excluding Black jurors from Brandley's trial (Badrei 2023). Likewise, it has been more than one hundred years since Joe Winters was lynched as an innocent man with no trial, and the town of Conroe has not recognized this injustice in any capacity. Around 2019, Jeff Littlejohn, history professor at Sam Houston State University, has communicated with the Montgomery County Historical Commission regarding memorializing the Winters's lynching. In no uncertain terms, the MCHC has expressed that they have no intention to ever erect a historical marker for the Winters lynching or any other lynchings in the county (personal interview). As a result, Littlejohn has formed the Montgomery County Remembrance Committee (MCRC) with the EJI (April is a member). The MCRC plans to craft a historical marker that memorializes Winters and makes a clear statement about the role of racialized violence in Conroe, Texas. Without organizations like EJI, there would be no ability to circulate information about Winters's lynching in a public venue.

The fight to remember local countermemories requires local people to enact change. Without the pressure from Littlejohn and the MCRC, the town would have neither the desire nor the need to recall one of the worst events in its history. But the pressure from these people and organizations makes the remembrance possible, even if it remains officially unsanctioned. When local and state officials often fail to sanction the memory of such wretched events because of fear of essentializing a community, local groups like the MCRC can act to turn absences into presences. We do not always have to rely on the state to act because the state often delays, postpones, and erases. National narratives of remembering and forgetting often have many institutions and high positioned individuals moving conversations forward. Smaller communities do not have this luxury.

On Acknowledging Wrongdoing and the KKK in Vidor

Growing up in Grand Saline taught me (James) quite a bit about racism and sundown towns. I learned to fear and hate Black people and learned that they were "worse" than me, on a racial hierarchy scale constructed by white people in the community. But even my hometown's racism was not the epicenter of acknowledged white supremacy. In my high school days, I learned about another town in Texas with a similar racist history: Vidor. Actually, in 2015, when I interviewed Michael Hall, a writer for *Texas Monthly*, about Grand Saline he told me that my hometown had the reputation of being racist, similar to Vidor. Where the racism in Grand Saline is based more on story and legend, Vidor earned its reputation through various high-profile racist incidents in the 1990s.

The history goes deeper, though. Black people were first driven out of Vidor in the 1920s in a racist purge, earning the community the description of "a Klan stronghold" (Swartz 1993). Decades later, the city of Vidor was a part of a desegregation lawsuit that led to the Orange County Public Housing Authority to attempt to desegregate the community's public housing in 1993. Two single Black women with five children between them and two single Black men moved into the presumably desegregated housing. They all left before the year ended due to the constant terror perpetrated by local white supremacist groups. Skinheads and the KKK marched through Vidor and held protests to stop the integration in 1993 and 1994. Even more blatantly, the KKK hosted its national office in Vidor for over fifty years. The history is embedded within the memory of the town. Today, there are still few if any Black people in the community, and the town's reputation persists across the entire state. Most Texans have heard of Vidor and its blatant racism.

Often, scholars think of countermemory as a way to grapple with the past, to come to terms with what a community does not want to remember. Obviously, Vidor does need to grapple with its very real racist history, but we also believe that being public about the KKK's terror and the town's pitiful attempt at desegregation in the 1990s could help the community move forward, even if many citizens reject the claimed memory. If Vidor truly wants to move past its reputation, would not a public marker—in a prominent position—detailing their history and wrongdoings serve that purpose? How could it garner bad press? Anyone searching for Vidor on the internet sees only one theme: the town's racism. Arguably, by never engaging communal discussions about Vidor's racist past, the town condones its own racist history. Residents accept it by not interacting with it. Absence in this case is approval.

There is local evidence for both of these premises—that an intervention can lead to reputational change and that if nothing is done, the reputation will stay the same. In summer 2020, some citizens in Vidor and neighboring communities came together to host a Black Lives Matter rally after the murder of George Floyd, with about 150 to 200 people in attendance, in Vidor's town square. Many articles were written about the event, with a major story published in *Texas Monthly* titled "Black Lives Matters Comes to Vidor—Yes, Vidor" (the title implies what all Texans know about the community), illustrating that perhaps progress had occurred within the town. This press coverage demonstrates how a Black Lives Matter protest generated positive news for the community and also how much the town's past sticks with it. Rhetorically speaking, it is hard to imagine how such press would further denigrate the town's reputation. Yet only a handful of residents participated in this event.

If the local city council and business leaders banded together to create a memorial that detailed the town's past and ended with a promise to do better, Vidor's public memory and reputation could change. The community would not just be marked as a bigoted place that hates integration; it could be viewed as a town that wants to change its reputation. All nonracists could support that. More importantly, the town would be viewed as *trying* to change. A countermemory, in this sense, could mark a move toward a better reputation, true healing, and possibly an ideological change in the community.

Yet, throughout American history, we have never found a memorial that performs such a function. These types of artifacts could exist in many different communities throughout the United States, in places of racial terror in the South, sundown towns in the Midwest and Northeast, and more. Not a single community has ever, to our knowledge, openly acknowledged its past misdeeds in a town memorial. I (James) have called for my hometown of Grand Saline to take such a measure multiple times, with no success. It seems that towns marred by their racist public memories could counter them with promises to do better moving forward, yet never do so.

Why? Is it the fear that such an acknowledgement will be used against them, marking them as an explicitly racist community (a fact that many already know and believe)? A public marker is not going to be the first discursive text to reinforce this perception: internet searches, private conversations, and the rumor mill keep these legacies alive. We cannot imagine a marker that admits this history, with a promise to do better, would generate worse perceptions about the town. It could only make the rhetorical situation better. So, perhaps the town's unwillingness to make such a promise is because some of the townspeople either want to be racist or want to hide behind their racism. The truth of the matter is, until towns like Vidor publicly decide to combat their history and public reputation, nothing will ever change.

What We Do Not Name in Jasper

On a hot summer night in Jasper in June 1998, James Byrd Jr., a Black man, attempted to find a ride home after spending the afternoon with his family across town, when he came across three white men, Shawn Berry, Lawrence Brewer, and John King, riding in a truck. He believed they stopped to give him a lift. However, their intentions were much more sinister. They carried Byrd to a remote area in the woods and beat him, spray-painted his face, and urinated and defecated on him. Hours later, the three white men tied him to the back of the pickup truck and dragged him for three miles on the outskirts of town. An autopsy conducted by the area medical examiner concluded that Byrd eventually died during the dragging, with his head being severed along the way. Soon, the small lynch mob dumped Byrd's body in front of a Black church. The event is recognized as one of the most brutal murders in Texas history and one clearly constituting a hate crime. All three men were arrested. Brewer was executed in 2011 and King in 2019; Berry received a life sentence with eventual parole eligibility.

Byrd's vicious murder quickly became national news. The NAACP and political activists like Jesse Jackson condemned the murderers in the press. Byrd's legacy was even featured in national legislation. In 2009, President Obama signed the Matthew Shepard and James Byrd Jr. Hate Crimes Prevention Act into law. The law expanded the definition of hate crimes—including adding the victim's sexuality and removing the prerequisite that a person must be engaging in a federally protected activity when the crime against them is committed. While many of the memories on the countertour in this chapter involve old stories, often taking place in decades or centuries past, Byrd's murder occurred only a quarter century ago. This might lead one to believe that Jasper would do more to honor Byrd's life and death because they could not argue his story was ancient history. But, as might be expected by now, the town did the bare minimum.

There are two points of remembrance of Byrd's life in Jasper. The first is Byrd's gravesite in the local cemetery. Byrd lies in an above-ground casket surrounded by a security fence with spikes. His grave has been desecrated twice: once, in 2004, by two white supremacist teenagers who were found guilty of criminal mischief (Associated Press 2004) and once again a few years later . Byrd's grave is traditional—only imprinted with his name, year of birth, year of death, and a short inscription: "my beloved son." Still, as the desecrations demonstrate, this site also serves as a memorial to the violence that white supremacists committed. On two occasions, bigots have subjected the grave to vandalism because it is a site that symbolizes resistance to white supremacy. The other marker of remembrance is the James Byrd Jr. Memorial Park, on the outskirts of Jasper. The park consists of a playground with a jungle gym, swing set, and basketball court; a pavilion; and a bathroom. It is better defined as a playground than a park. The sign at the entrance of the park reads, "James Byrd Jr. Memorial Park / Constructed in 1999 by the City of Jasper to better serve the needs of our citizens." Below the park title are the names of the mayor and city council people who approved the park's creation.

Neither of these sites recognizes the reason Byrd was murdered. On the surface this makes sense: his grave was created less as a symbol and more as a place to hold his body; there would be no need to enshrine him for eternity, especially for family. The playground also does nothing to recognize why Jasper should remember Byrd. Those who know his name might be able to drive past it and reflect on the evil committed onto his body, but for outsiders, younger folk, or generations growing up decades from now, there is nothing in this space for them to learn about Byrd. These people might pass by the park and think it is named after a benefactor or someone important in the foundation of the community, not a hate crime victim.

The call "to better serve the needs of our citizens" on the park sign is even more bizarre. Clearly this quote refers to the racism and terror that Black citizens face in the community, but by not naming it explicitly or rebuking it, the mayor and the city council members who support this memorial do a disservice their citizens and those who drive past the park. The marker does not indicate anything besides vague unity—a message that means nothing unless the town details what happened to Byrd. While this is an important space to remember Byrd, Jasper has not constituted a discursive *reason* to remember him. The town created a space for those who know the history to recall him, fondly or with hate as with the decertations, but there is no space to learn about him.

We cannot help but imagine what Jasper might look like decades from now, when people who knew and loved Byrd have passed. Will the markers and spaces they created honor his memory still? Or will the lack of context and naming leave generations to drive past with no recollection of why Byrd is an important part of the community's history?

The Negative Spaces of Countermemory

All these sites—or lack of sites—on our countertour demonstrate the values of each community. Some are beginning to name their crimes and histories, as with Waco, while others fail to acknowledge anything explicitly, as with Jasper. At the end of the day, what is said or not said demonstrates to countertourists what each community holds true. If they name their dead and explain why they are important historically, some reconciliation is being attempted, even if it is not perfect. If they do not have the courage to do so or use implicit language, then they would rather hide in the shadows of time than relate how their town has committed harm.

For countertourists, this tour is not always about what is present. By their very name, "counter" tours or ("counter" memories) focus on what is hidden (often thematically or historically, but it could be about literal presence too). Where most tourist industries focus on what is *there* (memorials, markers, houses, and plaques), our tour focuses more on space and absence. What is not being named at the park in Jasper? Where is the memory of the KKK in Vidor? Why has it taken decades to erect a plaque in Waco? This tour argues that absence is presence for countertourists. There is something to be said about going to a site and taking in the nothingness, understanding what a community wants to forget or hides out of plain sight. Sites of public memory call for engagement. Usually that looks like a person reading a plaque, taking in the significance of a statue or memorial, or participating in some discursive reading and thinking. But our spatial analysis in previous chapters illustrates that negative space also creates meaning. Taking in that negative space—the absences—can be just as powerful as engaging with more typical public memories. Both of us have had visceral experiences on this tour. For instance, the fairgrounds at Paris, where one is surrounded by an open field and little else, take you back to the horrific lynching of a century ago, imagining the cries and fears of Smith and the spectacle in which so many participated. A shrine dedicated to Smith would help create some form of change in terms of collective values, but the emptiness there now resonates and speaks without any literal message. Knowing the history and visiting these spaces creates new meaning via the absence.

This tour is a countermemory tour, and the one commonality between all of these sites are these negative spaces. Negative space always exists at sites of public memory—typically noticed in the area surrounding an object. Yet most of the countermemories we detail in this chapter solely consist of these negative spaces: there are not many plaques and memorials and when there are, they typically do not provide much more information or only exist after years of fighting local and state governments. Countertourists thus must make meaning from these absences. If countermemories are designed to challenge the status quo or hegemony, then when there are no physical sites of countermemory, our bodies and experiences can perform said challenges. Being in a space, remembering the tragedy that occurred, taking in the moment and the history—even when a community erases it or forbids it from being public—embodies this countermemory tradition.

Conclusion

This tour is the first of its kind: a trip around parts of East Texas to illustrate the elusive and constrained power of countermemories in smaller communities. We by no means view this tour as the definitive countermemory tour of East Texas;

there are countless stories buried within these towns and other towns that we could neither uncover nor access. Also, we chose to put Grand Saline and Slocum on the map but not discuss them in this chapter simply because we have devoted analysis to them in other chapters. As we kept digging through this research, we were continually surprised by what we found, but we were also moved by what we did not uncover. In most of the communities we researched, including Waco, Paris, Vidor, and Jasper, the stories were already known to us, but we were surprised that other towns we investigated also had similar stories—some more prominent or verified than others.

These countermemories across five different communities show themes of presences and absences, what we remember and what we forget, spectacle, the importance of naming history, and the significance of location. On its own, each countermemory, be it through memorials or constructed around a memory with no physical or embodied marker, adds value to our analysis because it demonstrates how pervasive and often unwanted such recollections are. But, collectively, they also demonstrate how communities dealing with racist histories systemically forget and erase these stories from their memory. It is much easier for most, especially white people, to let the past remain the past and to take firm stands on how towns have changed than remember racist lynchings and misdeeds, especially in our current era, when discussions of race have led to more people boasting that people of color are the true racists and any discussion of race should be erased (see terribly reasoned op-eds like Ben Weingarten's "Antiracism Is Racist On Its Own Terms" [2021]). But how informative is it for folks to not remember these crimes? It is easier, for sure, but for a people who love to cite the maxim "those who do not learn history are doomed to repeat it," some only want to remember a certain type of history, not the muddied truths of crimes and sins of decades ago. This tour, therefore, speaks against this modern ideological stance that disregards history, attempting to remind people of what they wish not to remember in hopes that such memories could be fruitful for them moving forward.

The tour is a journey we hope some might take as a historical, countermemory pilgrimage of sorts (even if only ventured digitally). While driving through all of these communities in a day or two would be too much, we imagine the tour could be covered in a few ways: as a trip that lasts four or five days or just taken one countermemory at a time. These sites are spaced out over hundreds of miles, through communities not often accessible by interstates or major highways. Arguably, that is what allows them to hide their histories more in the background—the lack of access to the towns, their archives, and their histories. But their lack of access means they need more attention. There are many ways to view these sites, by visiting the spaces where racial violence and murder occurred as with Paris and Waco or visiting memorials and markers at sites like

Jasper. Nevertheless, there is a unique embodied experience of taking in these locations in person—seeing what is and is not there—and taking in the air of the memories. Visiting these sites digitally via ArcGIS or Google Maps can still be fruitful, but it does not capture the overall experience (we understand this, though, as people who had to write much of this chapter during the beginning of the COVID-19 pandemic). No matter how you engage with these sites, it is simply important to participate in these memoryscapes—to bring back histories some people want to keep buried.

Conclusion

A REFLECTION AND A CALL

"Our action items for redressing inequalities should include: Recognizing . . . Revealing . . . Rejecting . . . and Replacing unjust and oppressive practices with intersectional, coalition-led practices."

—Rebecca Walton, Kristen R. Moore, and Natasha N. Jones, "Coalitional Action"

As we write this conclusion, conservatives have developed a new boogeyman-of-the-year: critical race theory. There have been many conservative boogeymen in the twenty-first century: Obama, "death panels" associated with the Affordable Healthcare Act, trans people, homosexuality, and the "hoax" of COVID-19. However, the particular CRT scare tactic comes at the tail end of the Black Lives Matter movement, born in 2014 with the deaths of Michael Brown and Eric Garner and reenergized in 2020 with the death of George Floyd. For many white Americans, race and racism are nonstarters, things of the past. In James Chase Sanchez's documentary *Man on Fire* (2018), the former mayor of rural Grand Saline, white man in his mid-fifties, talks about racism as being something of yesteryear, pre–Civil Rights. But even in this claim, he downplays the extent of racism. "You have to remember in the 1950s and 1960s," he begins. "Black people could not eat in many restaurants. People were mean to them. They had different water fountains." In this moment, the former mayor constructed racism in terms of segregation, which absolutely was morally wrong and despicable, but entirely erased the worst parts of the pre–Civil Rights era—lynchings, racist violence, and murder. The former mayor is not the only person who feels this way in the documentary or in society. Many white people gloss over the worst parts of America's racist history, making it more palatable for them in the present. If you make the past seem not as bad as it truly was, then you do not have to spend so much time today discussing it. The past can stay in the past.

Fast-forward to today, and the conservative diatribe against critical race theory is solely an extension of "racism really was not that bad back in the day." Many have lobbed criticisms that conservatives are not actually angry about critical race theory (most of the debates and public statements show an apparent ignorance about even defining the term); rather, this is just a deliberate attempt to erase the past. Supporters of the anti-CRT crowd would argue that our work on countermemories is solely intended to make white people feel guilty or to indoctrinate the masses. Such an accusation against anti-CRT conservatives might seem far-fetched, but when you read recent legislation being entered into state legislators—some of which has as of this writing passed into law—it is not. For instance, Texas House Bill 3979 prohibits the teaching of Nikole Hannah-Jones's *1619 Project*. Senate Republicans in Texas went even further by advancing SB 3, a bill erasing requirements to teach the history of white supremacy in the United States, including talking about slavery and the Ku Klux Klan (Baker 2021). Florida's education department blocked the inclusion of AP African American Studies in public schools in 2023, calling the course "a form of political indoctrination and a violation of state law" (Kim 2023). Florida's Education Commissioner Manny Diaz Jr. called the AP African American studies class "woke indoctrination masquerading as education," referencing Governor Ron DeSantis's Stop WOKE Act (Treisman 2023). While it may seem like only a handful of governors and state legislators are behind these anti-Black movements, these states are simply training grounds for other states to adopt similar measures.

Though we started this project before this contemporary exigence, the ongoing war on history illustrates the utter importance of our work. For many white conservatives in this country, countermemories are a threat to their identity, their politics, their ideologies. They are not interested in acknowledging or understanding the truth; they only want a vision of the past that supports their worldviews. Liberatory countermemory, by its very nature, challenges those who only want to accept a singular, American exceptionalist interpretation of American history. We need more of these types of memories—in discursive and nondiscursive texts—to keep the memory of a different history alive. This book is one way to push back against a public memory system that continues to dismiss and erase; there are many other iterations and examples. Yet, as scholars of rhetoric, we believe it is time to shift into action.

We both have a history of turning our academic inquiries into public-facing projects, especially ones based on countermemory. While studying countermemory in Pendleton, South Carolina, April worked with a local community nonprofit, the Pendleton Foundation for Black History and Culture, to create a digital/virtual countertour of the town's erased Black history. James created a documentary based upon his research and is working to erect a countermemory monument in his hometown. The issue of action is important to both of us.

Yet, turning countermemory into material artifacts—either ones listed in this book or ones found in places across the country—is uniquely based upon place and location. The more local the scholar, the easier to do this type of work in individual communities. We believe that more artifact-based scholarship can change how scholars and the public discuss countermemory. So, what does that look like?

First, we challenge more individuals interested in public rhetorics, public memory, countermemory, and associated subjects to continue to do this work of theory-building and local analysis. While our book takes a wide-sweeping view of liberatory countermemories as they play out in our home areas, the South, popular culture, mapping, and tourism, there are still countless implications for future scholars:

1. How do countermemory and public memory square off in the public sphere?
2. Historically, countermemory has prompted violence (as with the Emmett Till marker in Mississippi). What aspects of countermemory lead people to violent acts?
3. Has countermemory ever been transformed and accepted by local communities?
4. How do digital spaces and platforms influence the ways people interact with countermemory?
5. What is the future of the heritage tourism industry, as more Americans experience discontent with erased narratives and Lost Cause ideologies?
6. What do nonliberatory countermemories or countermemories against racial injustice look like?

These are just a few questions that we could imagine other scholars could explore. We hope that this book can bring forth a new wave of public memory scholarship in the field of rhetorical studies, especially as more and more scholars want to see their work having an impact in their local communities.

However, the work does not have to stop with the scholarship, of course. Rhetoricians can and should be front-and-center in helping these memories come to life by constructing public narratives, shaping tourism of these sites, building monuments, and so forth. Our call, then, is not just for us to "do the work" in terms of scholarship. It is a call to do the work in reference to the public interactions with and constructions of countermemory.

Most importantly, scholarship alone is insufficient if we expect lasting change in our communities. Ultimately, a rhetoric of countermemory is intrinsically linked to community engagement, which is something that both of us have endeavored to model in our work. While we have practiced countermemory scholarship beyond academia, we find that organizations like the EJI model a heuristic for community-engaged countermemory on a wide-reaching scale. We have already discussed at length how the NMPJ functions as a site of countermemory and even as a countermap of racialized violence in the United States. Though their impact is significant to the public memory landscape, EJI's Community Remembrance Projects (CRP) best illustrate the importance of community interaction within these conversations about race, racism, and memory. A CRP, as defined by EJI in their catalog *Community Remembrance Project: A New Commitment to Truth and Justice*, is a multipronged community engagement and education effort that "invites communities to engage in restorative truth-telling efforts to work towards repairing the harm caused as a result of an era of enslavement, an era of racial terror lynching and violence, an era of Jim Crow segregation, and an ongoing era of mass incarceration in our nation" (Equal Justice Initiative 6).

There are three components to a CRP: Soil Collection Community Project, Historical Marker Project, and a Racial Justice Essay Contest. While each aspect tackles a distinct area of public memory community engagement, taken together, they "clearly demonstrate how coalitions can tactically intervene in racist systems" (O'Brien and Walwema 2022, 52). According to EJI's catalog, a CRP is initiated first usually by a handful of local residents who, after deciding to form a committee, then consider what ongoing efforts already exist in the community (EJI 2021, 31). These early actions are considered "intentional community assessment," and "they serve to evaluate the dynamics within a community before introducing a CRP." This perspective contrasts with one that would seek to colonize community work that is already in place. It is also important to the EJI that committee members carefully consider the impacts of a CRP in local communities, and therefore, they highly recommend that each CRP includes Black residents who are relatives or descendants of individuals who were lynched. As a result, these community members who have lived through and carry the ancestral trauma of racial violence can share their stories as part of the research process. Ideally, these relatives lead or serve on a CRP and are at the center of community events, such as the unveiling of a historical marker or a commemorative march (EJI 2021, 92). As a true community organization, a CRP should comprise a diverse group of people, including school board members, students, town board members, university faculty, church members, and many others.

I (April) am a member of two local Texas CRPs: the Walker County Remembrance Committee and the Montgomery County Remembrance Committee. Walker County is where I teach at Sam Houston State University, and Montgomery County is where I live (a highly populated county just north of

Houston). My colleague in the history department at Sam Houston State University, Jeffrey Littlejohn, had previously participated in a CRP for Harris County and organized the Walker and Montgomery Counties' remembrance committees. Early in the process, we met with two EJI community partners, Keiana West and Kiara Boone, and in that meeting, they explained the underlying principles of a CRP as well as long-term goals. While the CRP consists of three efforts (soil collection, historical marker, and racial justice essay contest), these are viewed as one larger project to build relationships between EJI and the community and to promote open dialogue. The EJI partners were clear that 1) EJI has no desire to bulldoze their way into a community and force truth-telling efforts, and 2) the goal is for EJI to build long-term relationships within the community in the hopes that one day a duplicate monument from the NMPJ could be placed in the area. Clearly, EJI is concerned with a lasting community partnership; the community is "situated in a privileged position" instead of the opposite, where individual goals are a higher priority (Itchuaqiyaq 2021, 34).

As part of our work for the Walker County Remembrance Committee and the Montgomery County Remembrance Committee, we have completed archival research to uncover information about individuals who were lynched in these counties. From there, we needed to pinpoint the specific space where the lynching occurred. In the case of Joe Winters, who is discussed in the previous chapter, the newspaper images helped us in pursuit of this information. The images of Winters's lynching portray a building in the background with unique brickwork above the windows: this same building exists today. With this information, we hope to partner with EJI to get a historical marker placed to remember Winters's murder, as well as commemorating the many others who were lynched in Montgomery County. As could be imagined, the county has resisted any efforts to discuss racial terror violence—one member of the MCHC clearly expressed to Littlejohn that the county historical commission or state level historical commission would not be pursuing markers about lynchings (Littlejohn personal interview). With historical commissions like these and many around the country expressing similar sentiments, EJI's CRP, and specifically their Historical Marker Project, subverts the state apparatus, which desires to continue erasing the memory of racial terror lynching by completing funding and creating the historical markers for communities. EJI models how countermemory can be enacted with the help of communities; a CRP is backed by EJI but is a product of a community coalition. We provide this anecdote not to position it as the formula other scholars interested in this work should follow; rather, it is an example of how we can possibly intervene in local countermemory situations.

We close our book by looking ahead. As much as liberatory countermemory is about the past (trying to find the truth and uncover histories erased and forgotten) and the present (trying to connect said memories to a people who often does not want to remember the past), it is future-based, too. Countermemory is not a cure-all for society's woes. It cannot be. However, we do imagine what a future might look like in an American society that actually accepts and learns from countermemory. The crux of the memory problem/debate is that some people do not want to accept wrongs done in society because those memories do not fit their political ideologies or agenda. Thus, we argue about the best way to remember. But what if we collectively accepted our failures? What might that look like?

Present-day Germany is one example (though we are not comparing the atrocities of Nazi Germany to the horrors of lynching and the Confederacy). There are no statues honoring Nazi Germany or Hitler to be found in present-day Germany. Nazi symbolism is outlawed in the country, first because of Allied pressure post–World War II and reaffirmed by a German parliament vote against inciting violence in 1960 (Wildman 2017). Erik Bleich (2011) writes, "Germany acted more quickly in the postwar era to establish penalties for expressing or inciting racism. It did so in part through banning the use of Nazi rhetoric and symbols. Article 86 of the criminal code prohibits National Socialist propaganda that seeks to undermine the democratic order, while Article 86a forbids symbols such as Nazi flags, swastikas and the 'Heil Hitler!' salute" (920). Some with more conservative leanings might cringe at the word, "outlawed," but Germany took collective action: they understood the power of fascism to build forces of bigotry that would result in holocausts and never wanted to associate with that history again. Rather, Germany has focused its public memory artifacts on remembering the evils of the Holocaust, including the brass bricks called *stolperstein* ("stumbling stones") in Berlin's Charlottenburg district, "which are inscribed with the name—and details about the death of—people who once lived in apartment houses on Pestalozzi Strasse" (Westervelt 2021). While this movement began in the mid-1990s, there are now more than thirty thousand *stolpersteine* throughout Germany. The artist, Guenther Demnig, explains his reasoning behind crafting the *stolperstein*: "I think the large Holocaust memorial here [in Berlin] will always remain abstract. You have to make the decision to visit it," Demnig says. "But not with the stumbling blocks. Suddenly they are there, right outside your front door, at your feet, in front of you" (Westervelt 2021). Germans like Demnig look at the Nazi era as a lesson and decide as a nation to learn from it. Presently, however, there are signs that Germany's reckoning with its Nazi past is unfinished, especially as the Far Right's power continues to surge in 2024.

We are not calling for the United States to take a similar legal approach to the Confederacy or racialized massacres and tragedies; arguably, that fight would just lead many people whose identities are tied into a specific definition of "freedom" to double down on these associations. But what if we could still collectively learn these lessons by dissociating from Confederate memorabilia and other symbols of white nationalism and spending more time associating with our racial nadir? It is hard not to imagine how such a unity with our history could lead to unity surrounding present-day issues (the Black Lives Matter movement, vaccines, and climate change, for instance). At the end of the day, a shared understanding of our past is not just indicative of a mutual comprehension of history, it is the basis of a shared humanity, too.

Works Cited

AAG Call for Papers. 2018 American Association of Geographers Annual Meeting. Web.

"About the Museum." N.d. A:shiwi A:wan Museum and Heritage Center, accessed April 1, 2020.

"The African-American Monument." N.d. Go South! Savannah, accessed April 15, 2020. Web.

Ahmed, Sara. "White Men." *Feminist Killjoys*, November 4, 2014. Web.

Alderman, Derek. 2010. "Surrogation and the Politics of Remembering Slavery in Savannah, Georgia (USA)." *Journal of Historical Geography* 36 (1): 90–101.

Alderman, Derek, Joshua F. J. Inwood, and Ethan Bottone. 2021. "The Mapping behind the Movement: On Recovering the Critical Cartographies of the African American Freedom Struggle." *Geoforum* 120 (March): 67–78.

Amsden, David. "A Peculiar Institution." *New York Times*, March 1, 2015.

Armus, Teo. "Sen. Tom Cotton Wants to Take 'The 1619 Project' Out of Classrooms. His Efforts Have Kept It in the Spotlight." *Washington Post*, July 27, 2020.

Anreus, Alejandro. 1996. "Subversions/Affirmations: A Conversation with Jaune Quick-to-See Smith." In Jaune Quick-to-See Smith: *Subversions/Affirmations*, edited by Alejandro Anreus, 108–13. Jersey City, NJ: Jersey City Museum.

Associated Press. 2004. "Tombstone of Dragging Victim Desecrated." NBC News, May 6, 2004. Web.

Avery, Daniel. 2019. "A Visitor Did Not Want to Hear about Slavery on Her Plantation Tour." *Newsweek*, August 17, 2019.

Azaryahu, Maoz, and Kenneth Foote. 2008. "Historical Spaces as Narrative Medium: On the Configuration of Spatial Narratives of Time at Historical Sites." *GeoJournal* 73 (33): 179–94.

Badrei, Arman. 2023. "Clarence Brandley: Unjustly Convicted, Overdue for Justice." *Texas Observer*, March 20, 2023. Web.

Baker, Carrie N. 2021. "Texas Republicans to Ban Public Schools Teaching History of White Supremacy." *Ms. Magazine*, August 2, 2021.

Bammer, Angelika. 1982. *Visions and Re-visions: The Utopian Impulse in Feminist Fictions*. Madison: University of Wisconsin-Madison Press.

Barnd, Natchu Blu. 2017. *Native Space: Geographic Strategies to Unsettle Settler Colonialism*. Corvallis: Oregon State University Press.

Barton, Ben F., and Marthalee S. Barton. 2004. "Ideology and the Map: Toward a Postmodern Visual Design Practice." In *Central Works in Technical Communication*, edited by Johndan Johnson-Eilola and Stuart A. Selber, 232–52. New York: Oxford University Press.

Beck, Estee. 2015. "The Invisible Digital Identity: Assemblages in Digital Networks." *Computers and Composition* 35 (March): 125–40.

Bell, Derrick. 1993. *Faces at the Bottom of the Well: The Permanence of Racism*. New York: Basic Books.

Benjamin, Walter. 2006. "On the Concept of History." In *Walter Benjamin: Selected Writings*, vol. 4, *1938–1940*, edited by Howard Eiland and Michael Jennings, 389–411. Cambridge, MA: Belknap Press.

Bennett, Jane. 2010. *Vibrant Matter: A Political Ecology of Things*. Durham, NC: Duke University Press.

Berger, Maurice. 2012. "Lynchings in the West, Erased from History and Photos." *New York Times*, *Lens* (blog), December 6, 2012.

Berinato, Christopher. 2021. "That's So Savannah: Who Was Florence Martus, the Woman behind the Waving Girl Statue?" *Savannah Now*, June 23, 2021.

Bidgood, Jess, Matthew Block, Morrigan McCarthy, Liam Stack, and Wilson Andrews. 2017. "Confederate Monuments Are Coming Down across the United States. Here's a List." *New York Times*, last updated August 28, 2017.

Bills, E. R. 2014. *The 1910 Slocum Massacre: An Act of Genocide in East Texas*. Charleston, SC: History Press.

———. 2015. *Black Holocaust: The Paris Horror and Legacy of Texas Terror*. Fort Worth, TX: Eakin Press.

———. 2016. "July 29, 2010: Slocum Massacre in Texas." Zinn Education Project. Web.

B-lorenzo (@blorenzo). 2019. "Yup, McLeod plantation." Twitter, August 8, 2019.

Blair, Carole. 1999. "Contemporary U.S. Sites as Exemplars of Rhetoric's Materiality." In *Rhetorical Bodies*, edited by Jack Selzer and Sharon Crowley, 16–57. Madison: University of Wisconsin Press.

Blair, Carole, Jeppeson, Marsha S. Jeppeson, and Enrico Pucci Jr. 1991. "Public Memorializing in Postmodernity." *Quarterly Journal of Speech* 77 (3): 263–88.

Blakinger, Keri. 2018. "Wrongfully Convicted Ex-Death Row Inmate Clarence Brandley Dies, Months after DA Reopens Case." *Houston Chronicle*, last updated September 12, 2018.

Bleich, Erik. 2011. "The Rise of Hate Speech and Hate Crime Laws in Liberal Democracies." *Journal of Ethnic and Migration Studies* 37 (6): 917–34.

Bouie, Jamelle. 2017. "Government by White Nationalism Is Upon Us." *Slate*, February 6, 2017.

Boyle, Casey, and Jenny Rice, eds. 2018. *Inventing Place: Writing Lone Star Rhetorics*. Carbondale: Southern Illinois University Press.

Braidotti, Rosi. 2019. "A Theoretical Framework for the Critical Posthumanities." *Theory, Culture, and Society* 36 (6): 1–31.

Browne, Stephen H. 1995. "Reading, Rhetoric, and the Texture of Public Memory." *Quarterly Journal of Speech* 81 (2): 237–65.

———. 1999. "Remembering Crispus Attucks." *Quarterly Journal of Speech* 85 (2): 169–87.

Browning-Mullis, Shannon. 2022. In discussion with the author, August 31, 2022.

Buell, Spencer. 2020. "Someone Beheaded the Christopher Columbus Statue in Boston . . . Again." *Boston*, June 10, 2020.

Buncombe, Andrew. 2002. "Truth Hurts in a Deep South City's Tribute to the Shameful Days of the Slave Trade." *Independent*, August 27, 2002.

Burrough, Bryan, Chris Tomlinson, and Jason Stanford. 2021. *Forget the Alamo: The Rise and Fall of an American Myth*. Westminster: Penguin Press.

Butler, Tamara. 2018. "Black Girl Cartography: Black Girlhood and Placemaking in Education Research." *Review of Research in Education* 42:28–45.

Carmichael, Rodney. 2018. "Donald Glover's 'This Is America' Holds Ugly Truths to Be Self-Evident." Interview by Audie Cornish. *All Things Considered*. NPR, May 7, 2018.

Casey, Edward S. 2004. "Public Memory in Place and Time." In *Framing Public Memory*, edited by Kendell R. Phillips, 17–44. Tuscaloosa: University of Alabama Press.

Casey, Rick. 2021. "Did the Legislature Require Teaching 'Both Sides' of the Holocaust? Sort of, But They Were Just Kidding." *San Antonio Report*, October 26, 2021. Web.

Cixous, Helene. 1976. "The Laugh of the Medusa." *Signs* 1 (4): 875–93.

Clark, Gary, Jr. "This Land." 2019. YouTube video, January 10, 2019.

Clary-Lemon, Jennifer. 2019. "Gifts, Ancestors, and Relations: Notes toward an Indigenous New Materialism." *Enculturation* 30 (3): no pagination. Web.

Cochran, Elliott, and April O'Brien. 2024. "Mainstreaming Countermemory: Tracing Marginalized Narratives through Media Representations and Community-Engaged Memory Work." *Community Literacy Journal*.

Crampton, Jeremy W., and John Krygier. 2005. "An Introduction to Critical Cartography." *ACME* 4 (1): 11–32.

Coates, Ta-Nehisi. 2014. "The Case for Reparations." *Atlantic*, June 2014.

Cobos, Casie, Gabriela Raquel Ríos, Donnie Johnson Sackey, Jennifer Sano-Franchini, and Angela M. Haas. 2018. "Interfacing Cultural Rhetorics: A History and a Call." *Rhetoric Review* 37 (2): 139–54.

"Confederate Memorial Task Force Final Report." 2017. Savannah, Georgia (website), December 22, 2017.

Cosgrove, Denis. 1999. *Mappings*. London: Reaktion Books.

D'Angelo, Frank J. 2010. "The Rhetoric of Intertextuality." *Rhetoric Review* 29 (1): 31–47.

Daniels, Jessie. 2021. *Nice White Ladies: The Truth about White Supremacy, Our Role in It, and How We Can Help Dismantle It*. New York: Seal Press.

DeAngelis, Tori. 2019. "The Legacy of Trauma." *American Psychological Association* 50 (2): 36.

Deleuze, Gilles, and Felix Guattari. 1987. *A Thousand Plateaus: Capitalism and Schizophrenia*. Minneapolis: University of Minnesota Press.

Delgado, Richard. 1984. "The Imperial Scholar: Reflections on a Review of Civil Rights Literature." *University of Pennsylvania Law Review* 132:561–78.

Dickinson, Greg, Carole Blair, and Brian L. Ott. 2010. *Places of Public Memory: The Rhetoric of Museums and Memorials*. Tuscaloosa: University of Alabama Press.

Dickinson, Greg, Brian Ott, and Eric Aoki. 2006. "Spaces of Remembering and Forgetting: The Reverent Eye/I at the Plains Indian Museum." *Communication and Critical/Cultural Studies* 3 (1): 27–47.

Donald, Dwayne. 2009. "Forts, Curriculum, and Indigenous Metissage: Imagining

Decolonization of Aboriginal-Canadian Relations in Educational Contexts." *HAU: Journal of Ethnographic Theory* 2 (1): 1–24.

Doss, Erika. 2012. *Memorial Mania: Public Feeling in America*. Chicago: University of Chicago Press.

Douglas, Ron, dir. 2013. *Unseen Tears*. Buffalo, NY: Native American Community Services of Erie and Niagara Counties.

Druschke, Caroline Gottschalk. 2019. "A Trophic Future for Rhetorical Ecologies." *Enculturation* 28 (1): no pagination. Web.

Edbauer, Jenny. 2009. "Unframing Models of Public Distribution: From Rhetorical Situation to Rhetorical Ecologies." *Rhetoric Society Quarterly* 35 (4): 5–24.

"The 1811 Slave Revolt Memorial." N.d. Slavery and Remembrance: A Guide to Sites, Museums, and Memory, accessed April 3, 2020. Web.

Elliott, Debbie. 2015. "New Museum Depicts 'the Life of a Slave from Cradle to the Tomb.'" *All Things Considered*, NPR, February 27, 2015.

Eng, David, and David Kazanjian. 2003. *Loss: The Politics of Mourning*. Oakland: University of California Press.

Equal Justice Initiative. 2021. *Community Remembrance Project Catalog*. E-book.

"Explore Georgia's Historical Markers." N.d. Georgia Historical Society. Accessed April 23, 2020. Web.

Foote, Kenneth. 2003. *Shadowed Ground: America's Landscapes of Violence and Tragedy*. Austin: University of Texas Press.

Foucault, Michel. 1977. "Nietzsche, Genealogy, History." In *Language, Counter-Memory, Practice: Selected Essays and Interviews*, edited by Michel Foucault Donald Bouchard, 76–100. Ithaca, NY: Cornell University Press.

Franklin, Jonathan. 2023. "A Monument of Harriet Tubman Now Replaces a Statue of Christopher Columbus in Newark." NPR, March 13, 2023.

Gambino, Childish. 2018. "This Is America." YouTube video, May 6, 2018.

Garneni, Tanvi. 2020. "The Duality of the Black American Experience." *Bookends Review*, September 2, 2020. Web.

"The Georgia Civil Rights Trail: The Savannah Protest Movement." N.d. Georgia Historical Society, accessed April 23, 2020. Web.

Giorgis, Hannah. 2018. "Donald Glover's Evolving Vision of Black Kinship." *Atlantic*, May 11, 2018.

Gonzales-Day, Ken. 2006. *Erased Lynchings*. New York's Cue Art Foundation, 2006.

———. 2021. "Projects: Erased Lynchings." Ken Gonzales-Day (website).

Graff, Gilda. 2014. "The Intergenerational Trauma of Slavery and Its Aftermath." *Journal of Psychohistory* 41 (3): 181–97.

Gries, Laurie. 2015. *Still Life with Rhetoric: A New Materialist Approach for Visual Rhetorics*. Logan: Utah State University Press.

Griffith, D. W., dir. *The Birth of a Nation*. David W. Griffith Corp., 1915.

Gruenewald, Tim. 2021. *Curating America's Painful Past: Memory, Museums, and the National Imagination*. Lawrence: University Press of Kansas.

Hains, Tim. 2019. "Gingrich: 'Propaganda' for NYT's '1619 Project' to Claim American Revolution Was about Protecting Slavery." *Real Clear Politics*, August 19, 2019.

Hall, Michael. 2018. "'He Never Got an Apology': Death Row Exoneree Clarence Brandley Dies at 66." *Texas Monthly*, September 10, 2018. Web.

Hanna, Stephen P., Perry L. Carter, Amy E. Potter, Candace Forbes Bright, Derek A. Alderman, E. Arnold Modlin, and David L. Butler. 2019. "Following the Story: Narrative Mapping as a Mobile Method for Tracking and Interrogating Spatial Narratives." *Journal of Heritage Tourism* 14 (1): 1–18.

Harley, J. B. 2002. *The New Nature of Maps: Essays in the History of Cartography*. Baltimore: Johns Hopkins University Press.

Harris, Muriel. "Talk to Me: Engaging Reluctant Writers." In *A Tutor's Guide: Helping Writers One to One*, edited by Ben Rafoth, 24–34. New Hampshire: Heinemann, 2000.

Hawthorne, Camilla. 2019. "Black Matters Are Spatial Matters: Black Geographies for the Twenty-First Century." *Geography Compass* 13 (11): 1–13.

Hernandez, Brianna, and April O'Brien. 2024. "'Our Beloved Alamo': Racism and Texas Exceptionalism in Public Memory Systems." *Reflections* 23 (2).

Hiatt, Brian. 2019. "Does the Hooded Justice Twist in 'Watchmen' Honor the Comic Books?" *Rolling Stone*, November 19, 2019. Web.

Hunt, Whitney. 2018. "Negotiating New Racism: 'It's Not Racist or Sexist. It's Just the Way It Is.'" *Media, Culture & Society* 41 (1): 86–103.

Hurley, Elise Verzosa. 2018. "Spatial Orientations: Cultivating Critical Spatial Perspectives in Technical Communication Pedagogy." In *Key Theoretical Frameworks in Technical Communication in the Twenty-First Century*, edited by Angela M. Haas and Michelle F. Eble, 93–113. Logan: Utah State University Press.

Itchuaqiyaq, Cana Uluak. 2021. "Iñupiat Iḷitqusiat: An Indigenist Approach with Marginalized Knowledges in Technical Communication." In *Equipping Technical Communicators for Social Justice Work*, edited by Rebecca Walton and Godwin Y. Agboka, 33–48. Logan: Utah State University Press.

Itchuaqiyaq, Cana Uluak, and Breeanne Matheson. 2021. "Decolonizing Decoloniality: Considering the (Mis)use of Decolonial Frameworks in TPC Scholarship." *Communication Design Quarterly* 9 (1): 20–31.

Jackson, Rachel, and Phil Bratta. 2020. "Decolonial Directions: Rivers, Relationships, and Realities of Community Engagement on Indigenous Lands." In "Curation," special issue, edited by Ames Hawkins and Maria T. Novotny, *Journal of Multimodal Rhetorics* 4 (1): 50–86.

Johnson, Sonia. 1990. *Wildfire: Igniting the She/Volution*. London: Wildfire Books.

Johnson, Tre. 2018. "Donald Glover's 'This Is America' Is a Nightmare We Cannot Afford to Look Away From." *Rolling Stone*, May 8, 2018.

Jones, Arthur, dir. 2020. *Feels Good Man*. Sundance.

Jones, Natasha, Kristen Moore, and Rebecca Walton. 2016. "Disrupting the Past to Disrupt the Future: An Antenarrative of Technical Communication." *Technical Communication Quarterly* 25 (4): 211–29.

Jones, Natasha, and Rebecca Walton. 2018. "Using Narratives to Foster Critical Thinking about Diversity and Social Justice." In *Key Theoretical Frameworks: Teaching Technical Communication in the Twenty-First Century*, edited by Angela M. Haas and Michelle F. Eble, 241–67. Logan: Utah State University Press.

Jorgensen-Earp, Cheryl R., and Lori A. Lanzilotti. 1998. "Public Memory and Private Grief: The Construction of Shrines at Sites of Public Tragedy." *Quarterly Journal of Speech* 84 (2): 150–70.

Keller, Jared. 2016. "Inside America's Auschwitz." *Smithsonian Magazine*, April 4, 2016. Web.

Kim, Juliane. 2023. "Florida Says AP Class Teaches Critical Race Theory. Here's What's Really in the Course." NPR. January 22, 2023.

Kimmerer, Robin Wall. 2013. *Braiding Sweetgrass: Indigenous Wisdom, Scientific Knowledge, and the Teaching of Plants*. Minneapolis: Milkweed Editions.

King, Lisa. 2016. "Legible Sovereignties and the Tactics of Community Memory: Historical Mounds, Urban Places, and Reclaiming Native Spaces." Paper presented at the Rhetoric Society of America conference, Atlanta, Georgia, May 29, 2016.

———. 2017. *Legible Sovereignties: Rhetoric, Representations, and Native American Museums*. Corvallis: Oregon State University Press.

Kitchin, Rob, Justin Gleeson, and Martin Dodge. 2013. "Unfolding Mapping Practices: A New Epistemology for Cartography." *Transactions of the Institute of British Geographers* 38 (3): 480–96.

Koyer, Kalyn O. 2019. "'This Is America,' with References to Charleston Church Shooting, Makes Grammys History." *Post and Courier*, February 11, 2019.

Krakauer, Steve. 2023. "She Saw Trump Coming in 2016 Better Than Anyone. What Does Salena Zito See for 2024?" *Hill*, November 9, 2023.

Kwan, Mei-Po. 2007. "Affecting Geospatial Technologies: Toward a Feminist Politics of Emotion." *Professional Geographer* 59 (1): 22–34.

"Largest Slave Sale in Georgia History." N.d. Georgia Historical Society. Accessed April 23, 2002. Web.

Legg, Stephen. 2005. "Sites of Counter-memory: The Refusal to Forget and the Nationalist Struggle in Colonial Delhi." *Historical Geography* 33:180–201.

Levada, Olivia. 2021. "TikTok Star Uses Platform to Push for Historical Marker to Get Erected Recognizing 1916 Lynching of Jesse Washington in Waco." *Spectrum News 1*, July 8, 2021.

Levin, Brian. 2019. "Why White Supremacist Attacks Are on the Rise, Even in Surprising Places." *Time Magazine*, March 21, 2019.

Lindelof, Damon, dir. 2014–2017. *The Leftovers*. HBO.

———. 2019. *Watchmen*. HBO.

Lindmark, Sarah A. 2019. "'Watching Their Souls Speak': Interpreting the New Music Videos of Childish Gambino, Kendrick Lamar, and Beyoncé Knowles-Carter." MFA thesis, University of California, Irvine.

Littlejohn, Jeff. 2021. Personal interview by April O'Brien. January 14, 2021. Zoom.

Loewen, James. 1999. *Lies across America: What Our Historic Sites Get Wrong*. New York: Simon and Schuster.

———. 2005. *Sundown Towns: A Hidden Dimension of American Racism*. New York: Simon and Schuster.

Loften, Adam, and Emmanuel Vaughan-Lee. N.d. "Counter Mapping." *Emergence Magazine*. Accessed April 15, 2019. Web.

Lowndes, Coleman. 2017. "How Southern Socialites Rewrote Civil War History." *Vox*, October 25, 2017.

Lynching in Texas Staff. N.d. "Lynching of Joe Winters." Lynching in Texas. Web.

Martin, Michael, Dustin DeSoto, and Amanda Morris. 2019. "Racism in American

South Inspired Gary Clark Jr.'s 'This Land.'" NPR, *All Things Considered*, February 23, 2019.

Mason, Betsy. 2018. "Why Your Mental Map of the World Is (Probably) Wrong." *National Geographic*, November 16, 2018.

Massey, Doreen. 2005. *For Space*. Thousand Oaks, CA: Sage Publications.

McKittrick, Katherine. 2011. "On Plantations, Prisons, and a Black Sense of Place." *Social and Cultural Geography* 18 (8): 947–63.

McKrittick, Katherine, and Klyde Woods. 2007. *Black Geographies and the Politics of Place*. Boston: South End Press.

"Mission Statement." N.d. Marshall Project, accessed February 23, 2020. Web.

Monroe, Stephen. 2021. *Heritage and Hate: Old South Rhetoric at Southern Universities*. Tuscaloosa: University of Alabama Press.

Mzezewa, Tariro. 2019. "Elegant Lives Built on the Backs of Slaves." *New York Times*, June 30, 2019.

NAACP. 1919. *Thirty Years of Lynching in the United States, 1889–1919*. Clark, NJ: Lawbook Exchange.

Nelson, John. N.d. "Misconceptions: Some Common Geographic Mental Misplacements." Esri Storymaps, accessed November 17, 2020. Web.

Nora, Pierre. 1989. "Between Memory and History: Les Lieux de Mémoire." *Représentations* 26 (Spring): 7–25.

O'Brien, April. 2019. "Composing Counter-Memories: Using Memorial and Community Engagement to Disrupt Dominant Narratives." PhD diss., Clemson University.

———. 2020a. "(Digital) Objects with Thing-Power: A New Materialist Perspective of Spaces, Places, and Public Memory." *Trace*4 (March 11, 2020). Web.

———. 2020b. "Mapping and/as Remembering: Chora/graphy as a Critical Spatial Method-Methodology." *enculturation* 31: no pagination. Web..

———. 2021. "Exclusionary Public Memory Documents: Orientating Historical Marker Texts within a Technical Communication Framework." *Technical Communication Quarterly* 31(2): 111–25.

———. 2023. "Mundane Documents, American Exceptionalism, and Savannah's 'Unique' History." *Technical Communication and Social Justice* 1 (2): 1–27.

O'Brien, April, and James Chase Sanchez. 2021. "Racial Countermemory: Tourism, Spatial Design, and Hegemonic Remembering." *Journal of Multimodal Rhetoric* 5 (2): 4–26.

O'Brien, April, and Josephine Walwema. 2022."Countering Dominant Narratives in Public Memory." *Technical Communication* 69 (3): 40–55.

Ore, Ersula. 2019. *Lynching: Violence, Rhetoric, and American Identity*. Jackson: University Press of Mississippi.

Perea, Juan F. 1997. "The Black/White Binary Paradigm of Race: The 'Normal Science' of American Racial Thought." *California Law Review* 85 (5): 1213–58.

Phares, Gloria. 1998. "Appropriation Art and Copyright Law." In *Encyclopedia of Aesthetics*, vol. 1, edited by Michael Kelly, 70–76. Oxford: Oxford University Press.

Phillips, Kendall R., ed. 2004. *Framing Public Memory*. Tuscaloosa: University of Alabama Press.

Poirot, Kristan, and Shevaun Watson. 2015. "Memories of Freedom and White Resilience: Place, Tourism, and Urban Slavery." *Rhetoric Society Quarterly* 45 (2): 91–116.

Polus, Sarah. 2022. "Partisan Split Highlighted in Celebrations of Indigenous People's Day, Columbus Day." *Hill*, October 10, 2022. Web.

Powell, Malea. 2012. "2012 CCCC Chair's Address: Stories Take Place: A Performance in One Act." *College Composition and Communication* 64 (2): 383–406.

Propen, Amy D. 2012. *Locating Visual-Material Rhetorics: The Map, the Mill, and the GPS*. Anderson, SC: Parlor Press.

"Proud Boys: Far-Right Group Becomes LGBT Trend Online." 2020. BBC, October 5, 2020.

Quintilian. 2010. *Institutes of Oratory*. Edited by L. Honeycutt, translated by J. S. Watson. Ames: Iowa State University Press.

Radcliffe, Sarah A. 2011. "Third Space, Abstract Space and Coloniality: National and Subaltern Cartography in Ecuador." In *Postcolonial Spaces: The Politics of Place in Contemporary Culture*, edited by Andrew Teverson and Sarah Upstone, 129–45. New York: Palgrave Macmillan.

Rader, Dean. 2011. *Engaged Resistance: American Indian Art, Literature, and Film from Alcatraz to the Nmai*. Austin: University of Texas Press.

Rakoff, Vivian. 1966. "The Long Term Effects of the Concentration Camp Experience." *Viewpoints* 1:17–22.

Rao, Sonia. 2018. "'This Is America': Breaking Down Childish Gambino's Powerful New Music Video." *Washington Post*, May 9, 2018.

Reyes, G. Mitchell. 2010. *Public Memory, Race, and Ethnicity*. Newcastle upon Tyne, UK: Cambridge Scholars Press.

Reynolds, Nedra. 2004. *Geographies of Writing: Inhabiting Places and Encountering Difference*. Carbondale: Southern Illinois University Press.

Rickert, Thomas. 2013. *Ambient Rhetoric: The Attunements of Rhetorical Beings*. Pittsburgh: University of Pittsburgh Press.

Riley-Mukavetz, Andrea. 2020. "Developing a Relational Scholarly Practice: Snakes, Dreams, and Grandmothers." *College Composition and Communication* 71 (4): 545–65.

Ríos, Gabriela Raquel. 2019. "Andean Relational Ontologies." In Sackey et al., "Perspectives on Cultural and Posthumanist Rhetoric," 384–85.

Rosenfeld, Paul. 2015. "Why America Needs a Slavery Museum." *Atlantic*, August 25, 2015. Documentary.

St. Felix, Doreen. 2018. "The Carnage and Chaos of Childish Gambino's 'This Is America.'" *New Yorker*, May 7, 2018.

Sackey, Donnie, Casey Boyle, et al. 2019. Symposium, "Perspectives on Cultural and Posthumanist Rhetorics." *Rhetoric Review* 38 (4): 375–401.

Saegert, Rhiannon. 2023. "Jesse Washington Lynching Marker Ready to be Dedicated at Waco City Hall." *Waco Tribune-Herald*, January 3, 2023.

Said, Edward. 1994. *Culture and Imperialism*. New York: Vintage Books.

Sanchez, James Chase. 2025. "Beyond the Black-White Binary: Erasing/Composing the Brown Self in Rural Spaces." In *Nuestra America*, edited by Raul Sanchez and Iris Ruiz.

———, producer. 2018. *Man on Fire*. New Day Films.

———. 2020. "Public Memory Vs. History." Sanchez Facebook page, June 23, 2020.

———. 2021. *Salt of the Earth: Rhetoric, Preservation, and White Supremacy*. Champaign, IL: National Council of Teachers of English, 2021.

Sanchez, James Chase, and Kristen Moore. 2015. "Reappropriating Public Memory: Racism, Resistance and Erasure of the Confederate Defenders of Charleston Monument." *Present Tense* 5 (2): 1–9.

Sartwell, Crispin. 1998. "Appropriation." In *Encyclopedia of Aesthetics*, vol. 1, edited by Michael Kelly, 68–70. Oxford: Oxford University Press.

Sasse, Julie, and Jaune Quick-to-See Smith. 2004. *Postmodern Messenger, Jaune Quick-to-See Smith*. Tucson: Tucson Museum of Art.

Savov, Vlad. 2014. "Superheroes Don't Exist to Solve Problems, They Exist to Punch Bad Guys." *Verge*, November 20, 2014. Web.

Schwartz, Hillel. 1996. *The Culture of Copy*. Princeton, NJ: Princeton University Press, 1996.

Senda-Cook, Samantha, Michael Middleton, and Danielle Endres. 2018. "Rhetorical Cartographies: (Counter)Mapping Urban Spaces." In *Field Rhetoric: Ethnography, Ecology, and Engagement in the Places of Persuasion*, edited by Candace Rai and Caroline Gottschalk Druschke, 95–119. Tuscaloosa: University of Alabama Press.

Serwer, Adam. 2019. "White Nationalism's Deep American Roots." *Atlantic*, April 15, 2019.

Sharpe, Christina. 2016. *In the Wake: On Blackness and Being*. Durham, NC: Duke University Press.

Shugart, Helene A. 1997. "Counterhegemonic Acts: Appropriation as a Feminist Rhetorical Strategy." *Quarterly Journal of Speech* 83 (2): 210–29.

Sibley, David. 1995. *Geographies of Exclusion: Society and Difference in the West*. London: Routledge.

Silverstein, Jake. 2019. "Why We Published the 1619 Project." *New York Times*, December 20, 2019.

Simpson, Mark. 2004. "Archiving Hate: Lynching Postcards at the Limit of Social Circulation." *English Studies in Canada* 30 (1): 17–38.

Singer, Marc. 2002. "'Black Skins' and White Masks: Comic Books and the Secret of Race." *African American Review* 36 (1): 107–19.

Skeets, Jake. 2020. "The Memory Field: Musings on the Diné Perspective of Time, Memory, and Land." *Emergence Magazine*. Web.

"Smithsonian to Display Emmett Till Historical Marker." 2021. Smithsonian, August 27, 2021. Web.

Soja, Edward. 1996. *Thirdspace: Journeys to Los Angeles and Other Real-and-Imagined Places*. Oxford: Blackwell Publishing.

———. 2010. *Seeking Spatial Justice*. Minneapolis: University of Minnesota Press.

Stockman, Farah. 2018. "Monticello Finally Opens Door into the Life of Sally Hemings." *New York Times*, June 17, 2018.

Sturken, Marita, and Lisa Cartwright. 2001. *Practices of Looking: An Introduction to Visual Culture*. Oxford, UK: Oxford University Press.

Sundberg, Juanita. 2013. "Decolonizing Posthumanist Geographies." *Cultural Geographies* 21 (1): 33–47.

Swartz, Mimi. 1993. "Vidor in Black and White." *Texas Monthly*, December 1993.

Takei, George [@GeorgeTakei]. 2020. "I wonder if the BTS and TikTok kids can help LGBTs with this." Twitter, October 1, 2020.

TallBear, Kim. 2015. "An Indigenous Reflection on Working Beyond the Human/Not Human." *GLQ: A Journal of Lesbian and Gay Studies* 21 (2–3): 230–34.
Tell, Dave. 2019. *Remembering Emmett Till.* Chicago: University of Chicago Press.
Thrasher, Steven. 2017. "The Whitney Plantation Is the Only Confederate Monument We Should Keep." *Buzzfeed News*, August 21, 2017.
Todd, Zoe. 2016. "An Indigenous Feminist's Take on the Ontological Turn." *Journal of Historical Sociology* 29 (1): 4–22.
Towns, Armond. 2018. "Black 'Matter' Lives." *Women's Studies in Communication* 41 (4): 349–58.
Treisman, Rachel. 2023. "Florida's AP African American Studies Ban Should Raise Alarm Elsewhere, Lawmaker Says." NPR. January 23, 2023.
Tresaugue, Matthew. 2015. "In the Shadow of The Woodlands, Tamina Community Fights to Stay on Map." *Houston Chronicle*, October 17, 2015.
Tuck, Eve, and K. Wayne Yang. 2012. "Decolonization Is Not a Metaphor." *Decolonization: Indigeneity, Education and Society* 1 (1): 1–40.
"Two Negroes Lynched for Attacks on Girls." 1922. *New York Times*, May 21, 1922, 18.
Tyner, Judith. 2020. *Women in American Cartography: An Invisible Social History*. Lanham, MD: Lexington Books.
"Undertold Markers." N.d. Texas Historical Commission, accessed December 12, 2019. Web.
Vivian, Bradford. 2010. *Public Forgetting: The Rhetoric and Politics of Beginning Again.* University Park: Penn State University Press.
Walton, Rebecca, Kristen Moore, and Natasha Jones 2019. *Technical Communication after the Social Justice Turn: Building Coalitions for Action*. New York: Routledge.
Weingarten, Ben. 2021. "Antiracism Is Racist on Its Own Terms." *Newsweek*, May 7, 2021.
Westervelt, Eric. 2012. "Stumbling upon Mini Memorials to Holocaust Victims." NPR, *Morning Edition*, May 31, 2012.
"Who We Are." N.d. Visit Savannah. Web.
Wildman, Sarah. 2017. "Why You See Swastikas in America but Not in Germany." *Vox*, August 16, 2017.
Yancey, Kathleen, and Stephen McElroy. 2017. *Assembling Composition*. Urbana, IL: National Council of Teachers of English.
Zito, Salena. 2016. "Taking Trump Seriously, Not Literally." *Atlantic*, September 23, 2016.

Index

Page numbers in italics refer to figures.